Investment Management Certificate

Unit 1 – The Investment Environment

Practice and Revision Kit

Syllabus version 10.1

Contents

ISBN: 978 1 4727 0606 5
eISBN: 978 1 4727 0631 7

© BPP Learning Media Ltd – June 2013

Printed in United Kingdom by Ricoh
Ricoh House, Ullswater Crescent, Coulsdon, CR5 2HR

£45.00

Investment Management Certificate

Unit 1 – The Investment Environment

1. The Financial Services Industry

Questions

1. Within MiFID, which of the following is the responsibility of the host state regulator, for activities of a branch within the host state?

    A Conduct of business
    B Authorisation
    C Client assets
    D Capital adequacy

2. Which of the following instruments does MiFID cover?

    I   Transferable securities
    II   Money market instruments
    III Collective investment schemes
    IV   Derivative instruments for transferring credit risk

    A I, II, III and IV
    B III and IV only
    C I, II and IV only
    D None of I, II, III and IV

3. Which of the following is a method by which an overseas collective investment scheme may be authorised?

    I   Be based in a designated territory
    II   Individually apply to the FCA
    III Attain UCITS status
    IV   Become a member of the Overseas Collective Investment Scheme Association

    A I and III only
    B I, II and III only
    C II only
    D I, II, III and IV

The following relates to questions 4 to 9

An economic target of the UK government is price stability. To achieve this, the Government has set the target for inflation at 2%. If the annual rate of inflation falls below 1% or goes above 3%, then the Governor of the Bank of England must write an open letter to the Chancellor of the Bank of England.

4.   Interest rates in the UK are set following a meeting of

A   Debt Management Office

B   Treasury

C   Financial Policy Committee

D   Monetary Policy Committee

5.   The control of interest rates as a means of managing the economy may best be described as a key element of

A   Fiscal policy

B   Monetary policy

C   Industrial policy

D   Keynesian policy

6.   Were the government to adopt a policy of quantitative easing, which of the following would be correct?

I   The objective is to reduce the overall money supply

II   The central bank sells short term financial assets in return for money

III   Quantitative easing reduces interest rates from their current high level

IV   Quantitative easing is often characterised as Keynesian economics

A   I, II, III and IV

B   II and III only

C   III only

D   None of the above

7.   Faced with a 'double dip' recession, the Government announces that it intends to stimulate the economy by pursuing an expansionary fiscal policy. Which of the following would it be least likely to pursue?

A   Increasing government expenditure

B   Increasing the amount it collects in taxation with no change in spending

C   Borrowing more money so as to implement a road building policy

D   Maintaining current government spending plans while not reducing taxation

8.   The UK government must borrow each year to cover the amount by which its expenditure exceeds its income. This amount is known as the

A   National debt

B   PSNCR

C   PNBR

D   Current account deficit

9. **The form of the UK economy is best described as a**

    A   Mixed economy

    B   Free market economy

    C   Command economy

    D   Welfare economy

The following relates to questions 10 to 15

On 1 November 2007, the Market in Financial Instruments Directive (MiFID) was implemented in the UK. MiFID had been adopted by the European Council in 2004 and replaced the Investment Services Directive.

10. **Which of the following best describes MiFID Level 3?**

    A   The setting out of specific conduct of business principles

    B   The technical implementation of MiFID

    C   The need for MiFID member countries to implement rules

    D   The delivery of convergent implementation of the MiFID requirements across member States

11. **A number of organisations are excluded from the scope of MiFID. Which of the following would not be excluded?**

    A   Group treasury activities

    B   Operating a Multilateral Trading Facility

    C   Insurance companies

    D   Professional investors investing only for themselves

12. **The organisational and systems and controls requirements of MiFID and the Capital Requirements Directive (CRD) are implemented through a single set of high level rules known as**

    A   The common platform

    B   COBS

    C   The trading platform

    D   MTD

13. **MiFID is a European Union Directive and this means that**

    A   It may be addressed to a state, person or company and is immediately binding but only on the recipient (Regulation)

    B   Once issued, EU member state governments are required to alter national laws to conform within a specified period (Directive)

    C   It has the force of law in every EU state without the need for national legislation (Decision)

    D   Under the principle of subsidiarity, it may be adopted if a particular member state believes it will be beneficial

14. Within which geographic region may member firms use domestic authorisation to passport core investment business, under the terms of MiFID?

A   EEA
B   EU
C   EEC
D   EA

15. Which of the following financial instruments would not be covered under the terms of MiFID?

A   Units in a unit trust investing in bonds
B   Treasury bills
C   A contract of insurance
D   A futures contract based upon snowfall

16. Which of the following type of firm is outside the 'common platform' of SYSC provisions?

A   Independent financial advisers
B   Fund managers
C   Credit unions
D   Insurers

17. Which of the following is not part of the role of ESMA?

A   Working with the EBA and EIOPA
B   Establishing the FCA and PRA
C   Continuing the work of the CESR
D   Prohibiting financial products that threaten financial stability

18. The European Market Infrastructure Regulation (EMIR) comprises a set of standards for all of the following, except which one?

A   Trade repositories
B   Central counterparties
C   Equities settlement systems
D   Over-the-counter derivatives

19. Which of the following are core purposes of the Bank of England?

    I   Promoting effective competition
    II   Monetary stability
    III   Financial stability

A   I only
B   I and II only
C   II and III only
D   I, II and III

Answers

1. **A**   Where a branch is set up, host state rules will apply for operational matters

    See Chapter 1 Section 5.3 of your Study Text

2. **C**   MiFID does not apply to collective investment schemes

    See Chapter 1 Section 4.4 of your Study Text

3. **B**   A fund based in a designated territory (Channel Islands, Isle of Man and Bermuda) can be freely marketed in the UK as can UCITS funds and funds individually authorised by the FCA

    See Chapter 1 Section 6 of your Study Text

4. **D**   The Monetary Policy Committee (MPC) of the Bank of England was given responsibility for setting interest rates in the UK

    See Chapter 1 Section 4.3.2 of your Study Text

5. **B**   Monetary policy is the area of government economic policy making that is concerned with changes in the amount of money in circulation. The key tools used are the control of money supply and the setting of interest rates

    See Chapter 1 Section 4.3.1 of your Study Text

6. **D**   Quantitative easing may be used to increase the money in the economy when the interest rates are at a very low level already. This is achieved by purchasing short-term financial assets from the market

    See Chapter 1 Section 4.3.3 of your Study Text

7. **B**   Increasing the level of taxation would take money out of the economy and if the government does not increase its level of spending to replace the reduced spending the effect would be contractionary

    See Chapter 1 Section 4.3.1 of your Study Text

8. **B**   PSNCR (Public Net Cash Requirement) is the term used by the UK government to describe this borrowing requirement

    See Chapter 1 Section 4.5 of your Study Text

9. **A**   The free market economy in which market forces are allowed to reign, with minimal State intervention, and of a centrally planned command economy, such as that of the former Soviet Union and other Communist-ruled States are extreme forms of economy. The term mixed economy is the best description of the UK economy

    See Chapter 1 Section 4.1 of your Study Text

10. **D**   Answers A and B refer to Levels 1 and 2 respectively

    See Chapter 1 Section 5.2 of your Study Text

11. **B**   Operating a Multilateral Trading Facility (MTF) is one of a number of investment services and activities which are core MiFID activities. The others are excluded from MiFID

    See Chapter 1 Section 5.4 of your Study Text

12. **A** The Capital Requirements Directive or CRD and MiFID are being implemented through the single set of rules known as the 'common platform'

    See Chapter 1 Section 5.6 of your Study Text

13. **B** Answer A is describing an EU regulation, answer C describes an EU decision

    See Chapter 1 Section 4.2.3 of your Study Text

14. **A** The European Economic Area (or the EEA). This includes all EU states plus Norway Iceland and Liechtenstein

    See Chapter 1 Section 5.3 of your Study Text

15. **C** Contracts of insurance will not be covered under the terms of MiFID

    See Chapter 1 Section 5.4 of your Study Text

16. **D** The only types of regulated firms outside the common platform are insurers, managing agents, and the Society of Lloyd's

    See Chapter 1 Section 5.6 of your Study Text

17. **B** Working at the European level alongside the EBA and EIOPA, and continuing the work of the former CESR, ESMA does not have a direct role in the UK regulatory re-structuring

    See Chapter 1 Section 4.10 of your Study Text

18. **C** EMIR comprises a set of standards for regulation of OTC derivatives, central counterparties (CCPs) and trade repositories

    See Chapter 1 Section 7.2 of your Study Text

19. **C** Promoting effective competition is one of the operational objectives of the FCA

    See Chapter 1 Section 2.12 of your Study Text

2. Financial Markets

Questions

1.   The Bank of England has responsibility for the supervision of all of the following, except which one?

   A   ICAP Securities and Derivatives Exchange Limited

   B   European Central Counterparty Ltd

   C   Euroclear UK & Ireland Limited

   D   LCH.Clearnet Limited

2.   Which of the following are correct with regards to proxies?

   I   A proxy has the right to speak in a general meeting.

   II   A proxy may vote on a show of hands.

   III   A proxy may vote on a poll.

   A   III only

   B   I and II only

   C   II and III only

   D   I, II and III

3.   Which of the following are conditions for listing, according to the UKLA Listing Rules?

   I   The expected market value of shares must be at least £700,000

   II   Shares must be freely transferable

   III   Accounts must have been approved by an auditor for at least the last five years

   IV   Under normal circumstances, at least 25% of the shares must, at the time of admission, be in the hands of the public

   A   I, II and IV only

   B   II, III and IV only

   C   II and IV only

   D   I, II, III and IV

4.   How long after the half-year must interim results be produced for a listed company?

   A   One month

   B   Six months

   C   Two months

   D   Four months

5.   **The Disclosure and Transparency Rules (DTR) imposes various requirements. Which of the following is not such a requirement?**

A   Require directors of listed companies to report transactions in shares of the company

B   Impose obligations on listed companies to keep shareholders informed of price-sensitive information

C   Impose disclosure requirements in cases where there is suspicion of money laundering or terrorist financing

D   Impose notification requirements on major shareholders of listed companies

6.   **When an individual acquires a material interest in a company, the company should be notified of this within**

A   One business day

B   Two business days

C   Three business days

D   Four business days

7.   **How many days' notice is usually required for a General Meeting of a company where a special resolution is to be passed?**

A   7 calendar days

B   14 calendar days

C   21 calendar days

D   28 calendar days

8.   **How many shareholders must be present at an AGM to pass a valid resolution?**

A   Two persons personally present or their proxies

B   Five persons personally present or their proxies

C   Ten persons personally present or their proxies

D   Twenty persons personally present or their proxies

9.   **A shareholder who owns 17½% of the shares of ABC plc, a listed company, sells part of his shareholding, leaving a holding after the sale of 16½%. What disclosure obligations does the shareholder have?**

    I   Disclose the sale to the company concerned within two business days

    II   Disclose the sale to the company concerned by noon the next day

    III   Disclose the sale to the market via a Regulated Information Service within two business days

    IV   Disclose the sale to the market via a Regulated Information Service by noon the next day

A   I only

B   I and IV only

C   II only

D   II and III only

10. **Which of the following is not one of the recognition requirements applying to an investment exchange?**

    A There must be complaints investigation and resolution arrangements

    B The exchange must be authorised to conduct regulated activities

    C The exchange must have financial resources sufficient for the proper performance of its functions

    D The exchange must have rules covering default by an exchange member

11. **Which of the following bodies is responsible for considering applications by a company for its shares to be listed?**

    A The London Stock Exchange

    B The Department for Business, Innovation and Skills

    C Financial Conduct Authority

    D Her Majesty's Treasury

12. **How is price-sensitive information disseminated by companies who are listed on the London Stock Exchange?**

    A Through the press

    B Through the analysts of securities houses

    C Through a Regulated Information Service

    D Through the Annual Report

The following relates to questions 13 and 14

Shearer plc is a medium sized company which intends to have a listing on the Alternative Investment Market. It is hoping to raise £1,500,000 by issuing ordinary share capital. Because the company is not very well known, it is not expected to be a very liquid stock when traded but will be held by a small number of qualified investors.

13. **Given that the company intends to list on AIM, what is the least market value of shares that the company could have offered?**

    A £200,000

    B £700,000

    C £7,000,000

    D No minimum

14. **The AIM listing proves to be successful. However, two years later the company has a dispute with their NOMAD and the NOMAD ceases to work for the company. What action will be taken regarding the company as a result if they fail to appoint a replacement NOMAD?**

    A Listing will be suspended

    B No action will be taken

    C The firm will be de-listed

    D The NOMAD will be fined

15. **Which one of the following is not a requirement for a company listed on AIM?**

A The company must have a broker

B The company must publish immediately price sensitive information

C The company's free float must be at least 25%

D The company must have an LSE-approved NOMAD

16. **A firm issuing shares hopes that it will be able to avoid the need for a prospectus and hence save money. This could be because the firm**

A Is medium-sized

B Is raising only £1,500,000 in this issue

C Is not well known

D Is making the offer only to qualified investors

17. **The ordinary shares of Abercombe Fookes plc, a company listed on the London Stock Exchange, have been traded in high volumes in recent weeks. You have been asked to check if all the required disclosures have been made where individual shareholdings have changed.**

   The shares all carry the same voting rights. Which one of the following events concerning shareholdings in Abercombe Fookes plc must be publicised in order to comply with the Disclosure and Transparency Rules (DTR)?

A On 10 March, the shareholding of Greenhouse Holdings plc moved from 0% to 1.0%

B On 5 April, Brian Hewlett sold shares so that his interest in the company dropped from 2.9% to 1.7%

C On 21 April, Cranford Investment Funds bought more shares, moving their holding from 5.9% to 6.1%

D On 4 May, Streetford Capital reduced their shareholding from 6.8% to 6.1%

18. **Which body regulates the Alternative Investment Market?**

A The Financial Conduct Authority

B The Bank of England

C The London Stock Exchange

D The United Kingdom Listing Authority

19. **Which of the following is not a potential benefit of high frequency trading?**

A Lower transaction costs

B Reduced financial exclusion

C More efficient market pricing

D Improved liquidity

Answers

1. **A** ICAP Securities and Derivatives Exchange Limited is a Recognised Investment Exchange, while the other options are all Recognised Clearing Houses, which are subject to the prudential supervision of the Bank of England

    See Chapter 2 Section 3.1 and 3.4 of your Study Text

2. **D** Following CA 2006 changes, proxies may exercise all the powers the member would have if they were present in person

    See Chapter 2 Section 5.8.5 of your Study Text

3. **A** The company must provide three years of audited accounts to the UKLA along with other documentation at least 48 hours prior to the hearing to decide the listing application

    See Chapter 2 Section 4.2.1 of your Study Text

4. **C** Interim results must be produced within two months of the end of the half-year

    See Chapter 2 Section 4.2.1 of your Study Text

5. **C** DTR covers A, B and D, but not anti-money laundering disclosures

    See Chapter 2 Section 5.1, 5.2 & 5.6 of your Study Text

6. **B** A material interest is an investor who has a 3% or more holding in the company (aggregated with those investments of connected parties, eg spouses, infant child but not siblings). Once the investor reaches 3% and every time the investor changes the holding by going through a percentage point, eg 6.7% to 7.1% the investor must inform the company by the end of the second business day following the day of trade, ie T + 2

    See Chapter 2 Section 5.2 of your Study Text

7. **B** A special resolution involves a voting majority of 75% or more and would be required for certain major decisions, such as changing the company's name or undertaking a share buyback

    See Chapter 2 Section 5.8 of your Study Text

8. **A** In general, a 'quorum' is achieved when two members (or their proxies) are present

    See Chapter 2 Section 5.7 of your Study Text

9. **A** This relates to the major interests disclosure requirements under the Disclosure and Transparency Rules (DTR)

    See Chapter 2 Section 5.2 of your Study Text

10. **B** Running an investment exchange is a regulated activity (arranging deals in investments), but Recognised Investment Exchange status exempts an exchange from the requirement to be authorised

    See Chapter 2 Section 3.1 of your Study Text

11. **C** The UK Listing Authority is a function of the FCA, which is the 'competent authority'

    See Chapter 2 Section 4.1 of your Study Text

12. **C** Disclosures are made through a Regulated Information Service (RIS)

See Chapter 2 Section 4.2.2 of your Study Text

13. **D** If going for full listing, the minimum expected market value would be £700,000 of shares however since the company is to be AIM-listed there is no minimum value

See Chapter 2 Section 4.3.1 of your Study Text

14. **A** The NOMAD is retained to advise the directors once an AIM listing is granted. Should the company lose its NOMAD, it must appoint a new one (otherwise the listing will be suspended)

See Chapter 2 Section 4.3.1 of your Study Text

15. **C** Full listed companies not AIM listed companies must have 25% free float

See Chapter 2 Section 4.2.1 of your Study Text

16. **D** Following 2012 changes, qualified investors comprise the MiFID categorisations of eligible counterparties and professional clients

See Chapter 2 Section 4.5 of your Study Text

17. **C** The change must be publicised if the 3% threshold is crossed in either direction, and if full percentage points above 3% are crossed, again in either direction

See Chapter 2 Section 5.2 of your Study Text

18. **C** Although the UKLA (the FCA) regulates the Full List, the LSE regulates AIM, publishing the AIM Rules and monitoring compliance with them

See Chapter 2 Section 4.1 of your Study Text

19. **B** Reduced exclusion of individuals from financial markets and products will not stem from HFT, but the other options listed were all identified as benefits in the UK Government's Foresight Report

See Chapter 2 Section 1.9 of your Study Text

3. Legal Concepts

Questions

1.   **Which of the following terms is not an essential element in the formation of a valid contract?**

   A   Process

   B   Intention

   C   Agreement

   D   Consideration

2.   **Where a company has its affairs wound up leading to its dissolution, how is this best described?**

   A   Receivership

   B   Liquidation

   C   Administration

   D   Bankruptcy

3.   **Ben Schwartz has been discussing taking out a life assurance. With such a policy, which part of the contract constitutes the 'offer'?**

   A   An insurer's acknowledgement of receipt of a proposal form

   B   An advertisement in an insurer's shop window

   C   A postal offer of life assurance with a free gift

   D   A completed proposal form

4.   **To be a fully binding agreement, which of the following attributes does a contract not necessarily need to have?**

   A   Offer and acceptance

   B   Intention to create legal relations

   C   Consideration

   D   Expressed in writing

5.   **Which of the following is not necessarily a feature of the relationship between an agent and a principal?**

   A   The agent receives payment from the principal

   B   The agent has a duty to avoid conflicts of interest with the principal

   C   The agent must hand over any benefit to the principal unless the principal agrees otherwise

   D   The agent must keep what he knows of the principal's affairs confidential even after the agency relationship ceases

6. **An independent financial adviser who offers advice and recommendations to a client from a full range of products is acting**

    A   As agent of the client

    B   As agents of the product provider

    C   As an attorney

    D   As an appointed representative

7. **An attorney may be defined as**

    A   A person who has been given authority to act on another person's behalf

    B   The person who takes possession of the assets of a bankrupt and distributes them to creditors

    C   A person who is not mentally capable of handling their own affairs

    D   A person who signs documents on behalf of someone else but, in so doing, does not have the authority to enter into a contract

8. **An Enduring Power of Attorney that has not yet been registered**

    A   Cannot be changed but can be registered

    B   Is established under the Mental Capacity Act 2005

    C   Covers personal health and welfare decisions relating to the donor

    D   Is void and must be replaced by a Lasting Power of Attorney

9. **Which UK Act of Parliament specifies a 'decision-specific' test which assesses whether a person will be able to take a particular decision at a particular time?**

    A   Trustee Act 2000

    B   Financial Services and Markets Act 2000

    C   Mental Capacity Act 2005

    D   Financial Services Act 2010

10. **Minka wishes to register a lasting power of attorney (LPA) which would allow his brother to make decisions on his behalf in the event that he becomes physically incapacitated by a progressive disease that he is suffering from. With which body would he need to register the LPA?**

    A   The Financial Conduct Authority

    B   The Ministry of Justice

    C   The Office of the Public Guardian

    D   The Attorney General's Office

11. **Mr and Mrs Entwhistle are each liable as individuals for the whole of their joint mortgage. This is likely to be so because they are**

    A   Joint tenants

    B   Equal tenants

    C   Tenants in common

    D   Common tenants

12. **If one of two joint tenants dies, the property will automatically**

    A   Belong to the estate of the deceased

    B   Be inherited by any children

    C   Be held in trust until the death of the survivor

    D   Belong to the survivor

13. **A Bankruptcy Order could not be brought against**

    A   An independent financial adviser who is a sole practitioner

    B   A limited company providing security services to government

    C   A partner in a firm of solicitors

    D   A Member of Parliament

14. **Mr M. Patel has substantial debts and now and finds himself unable to pay a number of bills which are now due. A supplier who is owed £720 of unsecured debt is considering petitioning for bankruptcy to recover the funds. Lawyers looking into Mr Patel's potential bankruptcy are also examining the case of a company that is in financial difficulty and have been late in paying a number of outstanding bills. The court will not entertain the petition of the supplier. Which of the following is the most likely reason?**

    A   Mr Patel would need to have been in debt for at least three years

    B   £720 of unsecured debt is not a sufficient sum

    C   Mr Patel is a private individual and not a company

    D   individual creditors cannot petition for a bankruptcy order

15. **Hamid Bahri was declared bankrupt with a bankruptcy order eighteen months ago. Amounts due to creditors amounting to £15,000 have not been paid. Hamid then inherits £25,000 from a deceased aunt. How much will Hamid be most likely obliged to pay to his creditors?**

    A   £10,000

    B   £15,000

    C   £25,000

    D   Nil

16. **Which of the following is best characterised as the basic aim or aims of insolvency law?**

    A Balancing the interests of competing groups and encouraging 'rescue' operations

    B Absolving the directors from responsibility for the company's collapse

    C Protecting the shareholders and directors of the company

    D Encouraging 'rescue' operations and protecting the shareholders of the company

17. **Ainsworth plc is going into administration. Which of the following best describes the procedure?**

    A The purpose is to provide a better way of realising the company's assets than could be achieved by receivership

    B The administrator is in most cases appointed out of court by a debenture holder

    C The administrator is concerned principally with the interests of the secured creditors who appointed them

    D The administrator acts mainly in the interests of unsecured creditors

18. **A trust is established with a sole beneficiary. The beneficiary of the trust has the absolute and immediate right to both the income and capital from the trust. This form of trust can be described as a**

    A Bare trust

    B Lifetime trust

    C Charitable trust

    D Discretionary trust

19. **A trust is established which gives the income beneficiary of the trust the legal right to live in a property during her lifetime. On her death the property will be held for the benefit of the second class beneficiary. This form of trust can be described as a**

    A Bare trust

    B Simple trust

    C Interest in possession trust

    D Charitable trust

20. **A will is not invalidated by the testator**

    A Being a minor

    B Having a criminal record

    C Lacking mental capacity

    D Having been pressured into including some parts of the will

Answers

1. **A** The other three are the required for a valid contract

   See Chapter 3 Section 2.1 of your Study Text

2. **B** Liquidation means that the company must be brought to an end wit the Liquidator acting mainly in the interests of unsecured creditors. Bankruptcy applies to individuals rather than companies

   See Chapter 3 Section 4.2.3 of your Study Text

3. **D** A completed proposal form constitutes an offer in the legal contractual sense

   See Chapter 3 Section 2 of your Study Text

4. **D** A contract does not have to be in writing for it to be binding, although a contract to sell land (ie, property, including a house) must be in writing

   See Chapter 3 Section 2 of your Study Text

5. **A** Reward is not a necessary feature of the agency relationship, although it is often present

   See Chapter 3 Section 2 of your Study Text

6. **A** The IFA owes a duty of care to the client, and acts as his or her agent

   See Chapter 3 Section 2 of your Study Text

7. **A** The attorney, who is given 'power of attorney' to handle someone's affairs, has the authority to enter into contracts

   See Chapter 3 Section 1 of your Study Text

8. **A** The Mental Capacity Act 2005 replaced the procedure for setting up Enduring Powers of Attorney with Lasting Powers of Attorney. Pre-existing EPAs can still be registered, although they cannot be changed

   See Chapter 3 Section 1 of your Study Text

9. **C** The Mental Capacity Act 2005 specifies such a test

   See Chapter 3 Section 1 of your Study Text

10. **C** An LPA must be registered with the Office of the Public Guardian before it can be used

    See Chapter 3 Section 1 of your Study Text

11. **A** With the form of joint ownership known as joint tenancy, the survivor will automatically inherit the whole of the property. Each joint tenant will normally be liable for the whole mortgage

    See Chapter 3 Section 1 of your Study Text

12. **D** Joint tenancy means that the survivor inherits the deceased's share of the property, rather like a joint bank account

    See Chapter 3 Section 1 of your Study Text

13. **B** Bankruptcy applies to individuals, sole traders or partners but not to a limited company, to which corporate insolvency law will apply

See Chapter 3 Section 4 of your Study Text

14. **B** The court will not hear a petition unless the creditor is owed at least £750

See Chapter 3 Section 4 of your Study Text

15. **D** Following the Enterprise Act 2002, a bankruptcy order is generally discharged one year after the date of the order. As such, further payments do not need to be paid to creditors

See Chapter 3 Section 4 of your Study Text

16. **A** The basic aims would include controlling or punishing directors rather than removing their responsibilities, and protecting creditors rather than shareholders of the company

See Chapter 3 Section 4 of your Study Text

17. **A** A debenture holder may appoint a receiver via a court to work on their interests. Acting for unsecured creditors better describes a liquidator

See Chapter 3 Section 4 of your Study Text

18. **A** A bare trust is also known as a simple trust. The trustee has no discretion over payment of income or capital to the beneficiary

See Chapter 3 Section 6.3 of your Study Text

19. **C** This is an interest in possession trust

See Chapter 3 Section 6.3 of your Study Text

20. **B** A, C and D are all factors that may invalidate a will

See Chapter 3 Section 5 of your Study Text

4. Regulation of Financial Services

Questions

1. Which body has the power to commission and publish an independent review of the economy, efficiency and effectiveness of the FCA's use of resources?

   A   The Bank of England

   B   HM Treasury

   C   The Financial Policy Committee

   D   The Financial Ombudsman Service

2. Which of the following are categorised as a regulated activity and require authorisation?

   I   Arranging deals in investments

   II   Establishing a collective investment scheme

   III   Sending dematerialised instructions

   IV   Advising on investments

   A   I and IV only

   B   I, II and IV only

   C   II and IV only

   D   I, II, III and IV

3. Which of the following constitute a regulated activity as defined by the Financial Services and Markets Act 2000?

   I   Provision of investment advice

   II   Fund management

   III   Acting as an unremunerated trustee

   IV   Dealing as a principal (where not holding yourself out to the market as willing to deal)

   A   I only

   B   I and II only

   C   I, II and III only

   D   I, II, III and IV

4. **Which two of the following statements are true in the event that a regulated activity is undertaken with an unauthorised firm?**

     I   Any contract entered into is unenforceable by the unauthorised firm

     II   Any contract entered into is unenforceable by either party

     III The maximum penalty is an unlimited fine and a two-year imprisonment sentence

     IV The maximum penalty is an unlimited fine or a two-year imprisonment sentence

A I and III

B I and IV

C II and III

D II and IV

5. **Which of the following are exempt from the requirement to be authorised to conduct regulated activities?**

     I   Members of an RIE

     II   Appointed representatives

     III Members of Lloyd's

     IV Lenders of regulated mortgages

A I and IV only

B II and III only

C I and II only

D II, III and IV only

6. **Which of the following are specified investments as defined by the Financial Services and Markets Act 2000?**

     I $/€ options

     II   Classic cars

     III Investment trusts

     IV FTSE 100 Index futures

A III and IV only

B I, III and IV only

C I, II and III only

D II, III and IV only

7. **The following are all classified as investments under the Financial Services and Markets Act 2000, except**

A ADRs

B Life assurance policies

C Deep discount bonds

D Currencies

8. **Which of the following are investments under FSMA 2000?**

    I   ADRs

    II   CDs

    III Premium bonds

    IV   Bank loans

    A I, II, III and IV

    B I, II and IV only

    C I and II only

    D II and III only

9. **Which of the following would be regarded as carrying out an investment business under FSMA 2000?**

    I   Arranging deals in investments

    II   Advising on investments in a *Financial Times* column

    III Publishing a Tip Sheet

    IV   Giving advice on investments as a remunerated trustee

    A I, II and IV only

    B I, III and IV only

    C I and III only

    D III and IV only

10. **What is the maximum penalty in a Magistrates' Court for conducting unauthorised investment business?**

    A Six months' imprisonment or a fine of £5,000

    B Six months' imprisonment and a fine of £5,000

    C Six months' imprisonment or an unlimited fine

    D Six months' imprisonment and an unlimited fine

11. **The prudential regulation of UK fund managers will normally be the responsibility of**

    A The Financial Conduct Authority

    B The Prudential Regulation Authority

    C The European Securities and Markets Authority

    D The Bank of England

12. **Up to what percentage may a listed company make purchases in a target company as a result of a dawn raid, without being required to make a mandatory offer for the target?**

    A 9.9%

    B 14.9%

    C 29.9%

    D 49.9%

13. **What is the name of the UK pensions regulator?**

A   The Pensions Regulator

B   The Office for Pension Regulation

C   The Pensions Ombudsman

D   The Occupational Pensions Board

14. **Which of the following is not a permitted investment under the Trustee Act 2000?**

A   Overseas land

B   UK government securities

C   UK ordinary shares

D   Authorised unit trusts

15. **In relation to takeovers, which of the following statements is true?**

A   An offer must remain open for at least 21 days

B   An offer can be made to selected shareholders

C   Purchases in the open market during the offer period are prohibited

D   Partial offers are never permitted

16. **A listed company makes an offer of £2.00 cash per share for another company's shares and, during the offer period, buys some of the offeree's shares in the market place for £2.10. Which of the following will it be obliged to do?**

I   Take no additional action

II   Make an announcement of the purchase

III   Increase the offer to £2.10 per share for future acceptances

IV   Increase the offer to £2.10 per share for offeree shareholders who have already accepted the offer at £2.00 a share

A   II, III and IV only

B   II and III only

C   III and IV only

D   I only

17. **How is the Panel on Takeovers and Mergers mainly funded?**

A   By government subsidy

B   By a levy on share transactions

C   By a levy on all Stock Exchange transactions

D   By contributions from all firms regulated by either the FCA and the PRA

18. **Under the Trustee Act 2000, how much of a fund should be invested into gilts and other fixed income securities?**

    A There is no minimum

    B At least 25%

    C At least 40%

    D At least 50%

19. **One of the conditions for a merger to qualify for referral to the Competition Commission is where the merged company has a market share of more than**

    A 10%

    B 15%

    C 25%

    D 50%

20. **When a company attempts to take over another company, their aim is to acquire a controlling interest. Which one of the following percentages represents a controlling interest (legal control)?**

    A More than or equal to 30%

    B More than 50%

    C More than or equal to 50%

    D More than 75%

21. **A merger may be referred to the Competition Commission if the value of the turnover of the company being taken over exceeds**

    A £60m

    B £70m

    C £80m

    D £90m

The following relates to questions 22 to 24

Tiger plc has made approached the Takeover Panel and announced that it intends to make a bid for Antelope plc whose shares are currently trading at £3.53 per share. It has not yet made a formal bid but they are intending to make a bid of £4.00 per share. They have been acquiring shares over the past year, the highest price they paid being £3.95 nine months ago.

22. **Having announced that it intends to make a bid, how long does Tiger plc have to make the formal bid?**

    A 7 days

    B 21 days

    C 28 days

    D 60 days

23. **Which of the following is incorrect with respect to the Takeover Code (the City Code)?**

A The Code has statutory force

B The Code applies to all public and private companies registered in the UK

C The Code has six general principles

D When a shareholding exceeds 30%, the shareholder must make a takeover offer

24. **Under the terms of the Enterprise Act 2002, the potential takeover is considered to see whether there are any competition issues. In this case**

A An investigation may be triggered where the combined enterprise controls at least 20% of the goods and services in the sector of the UK market

B The combined turnover of Tiger and Antelope exceeding £70 million may trigger an investigation

C The Competition Commission has the power to impose fines

D There are no appeals against the decision of the Competition Commission

25. **Natasha is an adviser who is preparing a newsletter for distribution to high net worth clients at seminars and other events. There will be a section in the newsletter on the Trustee Act 2000. Natasha has had a first draft of part of these notes typed, as follows.**

'The Trustee Act 2000 widened the investment powers of trustees, overriding provisions which may be included in the trust instrument that would restrict how the trust's money can be invested. All trustees and their advisers need to follow the Act, which overrides any trust deed that may have been executed before the Act came into force. The Act allows trustees to delegate functions to agents, including their powers of investment.

'Under the Act, trustees can make any investment of any kind that they could as if the funds were their own, except for investment in overseas land.

'Under the Act, trustees must keep aware of the need for diversification and suitability of the investments of the trust. Trustees must obtain and consider 'proper advice' when making or reviewing investments, and keep investments under review.'

Which part of the notes is least correct and therefore requires amendment?

A The Trustee Act 2000 widened the investment powers of trustees, overriding provisions which may be included in the trust instrument that would restrict how the trust's money can be invested

B The Act allows trustees to delegate functions to agents, including their powers of investment

C Under the Act, trustees can make any investment of any kind that they could as if the funds were their own, except for investment in overseas land

D Trustees must obtain and consider 'proper advice' when making or reviewing investments, and keep investments under review

Answers

1. **B**   This is one aspect of the accountability of the FCA to the Treasury

    See Chapter 4 Section 1.10 of your Study Text

2. **D**   Undertaking any regulated activity requires authorisation unless exempt

    See Chapter 4 Section 4.6 of your Study Text

3. **B**   Unremunerated trustees and dealing as a principal are excluded activities within FSMA 2000

    See Chapter 4 Section 4.6 of your Study Text

4. **A**   FSMA states that the innocent party to the agreement will still be able to enforce the agreement against the other party

    See Chapter 4 Sections 4.3 of your Study Text

5. **B**   Only the RIE itself is exempt, not the members of the exchange

    See Chapter 4 Section 4.5 of your Study Text

6. **B**   Classic cars are physical property and thus not investments as defined by FSMA 2000

    See Chapter 4 Section 4.11 of your Study Text

7. **D**   Currencies themselves are not specified investments, only currency futures and options

    See Chapter 4 Section 4.11 of your Study Text

8. **C**   Premium bonds are exempt as they are products of the UK's National Savings and Investment Bank. Loans are only regulated as investments when mortgages. A CD is a Certificate of Deposit

    See Chapter 4 Section 4.11 of your Study Text

9. **B**   The primary purpose of the *Financial Times* is not that of giving investment advice. A trustee is only exempt if not being paid for his services

    See Chapter 4 Section 4.6 of your Study Text

10. **B**   The maximum is the worst case where both imprisonment and a fine are imposed

    See Chapter 1 Section 4.2.2 of your Study Text

11. **A**   The FCA is normally responsible for both conduct and prudential regulation of fund managers

    See Chapter 4 Section 1.6 (Chart) of your Study Text

12. **C**   A mandatory offer is only required when the holding reaches 30% or, in certain situations, the holding is already over 30% and the investor buys one more share

    See Chapter 4 Section 3.4 of your Study Text

13. **A**   The Pensions Regulator is the regulatory body for work-based pension schemes in the UK

    See Chapter 4 Section 7.2 of your Study Text

14. **A** The Trustee Act provides investment guidance where none is provided within the trust deed. It states that the manager has a duty of care and can invest anything except overseas land

See Chapter 4 Section 6.1 of your Study Text

15. **A** Any takeover must remain open for a minimum of 21 calendar days, hence Day 21 is the first closing date

See Chapter 4 Section 3.6.2 of your Study Text

16. **A** If a predator company buys shares in the market during the bid at a price higher than the offer price, they must announce the bid and revise the offer to this new price

See Chapter 4 Section 3.4 of your Study Text

17. **B** There is a £1 charge on all contract notes in shares where the consideration is over £10,000

See Chapter 4 Section 2.1 of your Study Text

18. **A** Under the default provisions of the Trustee Act 2000, trustees may make any investment of the kind that they could if the funds were their own, with the exception of overseas land

See Chapter 4 Section 6.1 of your Study Text

19. **C** The Office of Fair Trading will consider whether a bid is against the public interest based on the market share of 25%. This is the criteria to suggest that there will be a 'substantial lessening of competition'

See Chapter 4 Section 2.4 of your Study Text

20. **B** A controlling interest is where a company owns more than 50% of another company. If a company owns 30% of the shares, this is known as effective control, rather than legal control (> 50%)

See Chapter 4 Section 3.4 of your Study Text

21. **B** Or a combined market share of 25% as 'a substantial lessening of competition'

See Chapter 4 Section 2.4 of your Study Text

22. **C** Following an announcement the company must make a bid within 28 days

See Chapter 4 Section 3.5 of your Study Text

23. **B** The Code applies to private companies only in certain cases, eg where they have been public within the last 10 years

See Chapter 4 Section 3.1 of your Study Text

24. **C** Failure to comply with a request for information may result in a fine. Regarding Option B, it is the turnover of the entity being acquired being over £70 million that is relevant – not the combined turnover.

See Chapter 4 Section 2.4 of your Study Text

25. **A** Restrictions in the trust deed will override the wider investment powers provided for in the Act

See Chapter 4 Section 6 of your Study Text

5. The Financial Conduct Authority

Questions

1. **Which of the following are true of the Financial Conduct Authority?**

       I   Its staff are Crown agents

       II   Its Board members are appointed by the Treasury

       III   Its governing body is made up entirely of the users of investment services

   A II only

   B I and II only

   C II and III only

   D I, II and III only

2. **Which of the following is a means of obtaining authorisation to carry on investment business?**

   A Application to the FCA

   B Direct application to the SEC

   C Application to a DPB

   D Membership of an RIE

3. **Allowing a firm to undertake regulated activities is known as the granting of**

   A Authorisation

   B Legal consent

   C Exemption

   D Part 4A permission

4. **Which of the following is not a threshold condition for becoming authorised by the FCA?**

   A Custody of investments

   B Location of company's offices

   C Adequate resources

   D Fitness and propriety

5. **Which of the following are disciplinary measures available to the FCA?**

       I   A public statement of misconduct

       II   A maximum fine of £100,000

       III   An unlimited fine

       IV   Cancellation of permission

   A I, II and IV only

   B I and III only

   C I, III and IV only

   D I and II only

6. Which of the following is not one of the seven main blocks of the FCA Handbook?

A   High Level Satndards

B   Business Standards

C   Perimeter Guidance

D   Redress

7. Hoolihan Investments Ltd are registered in the UK and intend to offer investment advice for high wealth individuals and small firms. The firm currently employs twelve analysts who all have a number of years working for larger firms in the same sector.

Which of the following bodies is it most appropriate for the firm to approach in order to get authorisation to offer investment advice?

A   HMRC

B   The FCA

C   The Bank of England

D   The PRA

8. Which of the following is a threshold condition for authorisation that is applied specifically by the PRA and not the FCA?

A   Business to be conducted in a prudent manner

B   Appropriate resources

C   Effective supervision

D   Business model

9. Which of the following does not describe one of the 'pillars' of the FCA's supervision model?

A   Analysis of issues and products

B   Event-driven work

C   The firm systematic framework

D   Dual regulation

10. Which of the following are powers possessed by the FCA to enable its information gathering requirements?

I   To require appointed representatives to provide documents

II   To require that relevant documents be provided at a specified place

III   To require that the firm appoint an accountant to verify documents

IV   To require that the firm carry out a one off investigation and report back to the regulator

A   None of I, II, II and IV

B   I only

C   I, II and III only

D   I, II, III and IV

11. **Red Bush Investments is given Part 4A permission to offer investment advice but a period of 13 months passes during which it carries out no business in this field at all. It is also authorised deal on its own account which it continues to do during this period. The FCA becomes concerned that it should protect potential clients from receiving inappropriate advice. What would be the regulator's most likely action?**

   A Cancel the firm's Part 4A permission

   B Remove authorisation

   C Vary the firm's permission

   D Fine the firm

12. **In recent years, the financial services regulator has characterised its approach to supervision using the phrase:**

   A 'Inspections based' approach

   B 'Bank examiner' approach

   C 'Outcomes focused' approach

   D 'Compliance focused' approach

Answers

1. A   FCA employees are not Crown agents or civil servants as the FCA is not a Government department. Its governing body should contain a balance between users and practitioners

    See Chapter 5 Section 1.1 of your Study Text

2. A   The Securities and Exchange Commission (SEC) is a regulatory body in the US. An RIE itself is exempt from authorisation but membership of an RIE does not confer authorisation nor exemption from authorisation. A Designated Professional Body (DPB) does not grant authorisation

    See Chapter 5 Section 3.2 of your Study Text

3. D   Applying to do specific activities requires Part 4A permission. As a result of obtaining this, the firm becomes authorised

    See Chapter 5 Section 3.2 of your Study Text

4. A   Custody is covered by the regulated activity of safeguarding and administration of investments but is not a threshold condition

    See Chapter 5 Section 3.3 of your Study Text

5. C   There is no maximum to the fine. The only maximum fine to remember is £5,000 in the Magistrates' Court

    See Chapter 5 Section 5 of your Study Text

6. C   The Perimeter Guidance Manual (PERG) is a Regulatory Guide and is not one of the seven Handbook Blocks

    See Chapter 5 Section 2.2 of your Study Text

7. B   FSMA 2000 creates the authorisation regime for regulated activities such as offering investment advice. A firm of this size and type would seek authorisation from the FCA

    See Chapter 5 Section 3.2 of your Study Text

8. A   The PRA's Business to be Conducted in a Prudent Manner Threshold Condition is closely equivalent to the FCA's appropriate resources and business model conditions

    See Chapter 5 Section 3.3 of your Study Text

9. D   Dual regulation refers to the regulation of prudentially significant firms by both the PRA (for prudential regulation) and the FCA (for conduct regulation)

    See Chapter 5 Section 4.4 of your Study Text

10. D   Under sections 165 to 176 of FSMA, all are powers of the regulator

    See Chapter 5 Section 5.2 of your Study Text

11. **C** Given that the firm is investing on its own account without apparent problem, it is unlikely that the regulator will cancel the firm's permission. However, because the firm has not offered advice for over 12 months, the regulator is likely to vary the firm's permission to stop them offering advice

See Chapter 5 Section 5.3 of your Study Text

12. **C** The regulators' philosophy has been characterised as resting not *per se* on principles, but rather on judging the consequences of the actions of the firms and the individuals supervised: this is what is meant by outcomes-focused regulation

See Chapter 5 Section 4.4 of your Study Text

6. The Regulatory Framework

Questions

1. A professional client who is a large company has lost £80,000 (in respect to a derivatives transaction) owing to the negligence of an FCA-authorised firm that has now become insolvent. The client would be eligible to make a maximum claim from the Financial Services Compensation Scheme of

    A   £150,000

    B   £85,000

    C   £50,000

    D   Nil

2. How often must an authorised firm inform the regulator of all complaints received?

    A   Annually

    B   Twice yearly

    C   Monthly

    D   Daily

3. Which of the following is not a controlled function?

    A   Finance function

    B   Proprietary trading function

    C   Internal audit function

    D   Money laundering reporting function

4. Which of the following can the Ombudsman do?

    I   Require that the firm involved complies with a money award

    II   Make an award to cover costs of a complainant

    III   Make a money award of £125,000

    A   I and II only

    B   II and III only

    C   I and III only

    D   I, II and III

5.   **Which of the following will not generally be eligible complainants for the purposes of the Financial Ombudsman Service?**

A   Private individuals

B   Small businesses

C   Small charities

D   Eligible counterparties

6.   **If the outcome of an investigation by the Financial Ombudsman is accepted by the complainant, then it is**

A   At the discretion of the firm to comply

B   Implemented by the HMT

C   Binding on the firm

D   Binding on the customer

7.   **If a complaint has not been resolved within eight weeks, which of the following must be given to a complainant?**

A   Information about the Financial Ombudsman Service

B   Information about the Financial Conduct Authority

C   Information about the Financial Services Compensation Scheme

D   Information about the Office of Fair Trading

8.   **Within how long must a firm send a written acknowledgement of a complaint?**

A   Promptly

B   Five calendar days

C   Seven business days

D   Seven calendar days

9.   **To whom should an eligible complainant take his complaint first?**

A   The Financial Conduct Authority

B   Financial Ombudsman Service

C   The authorised firm

D   The Complaints Commissioner

10.   **Who funds the Financial Services Compensation Scheme?**

A   The FCA

B   The taxpayer

C   Authorised firms

D   The Government

11. The maximum claim that can be made for protected deposits under the Financial Services Compensation Scheme is

A £35,000

B £38,000

C £50,000

D £85,000

12. To whom is the Financial Services Compensation Scheme (FSCS) directly accountable?

A The FCA and HMT

B HMT

C The Lord Chancellor

D The Governor of the Bank of England

13. Under which Act is money laundering an offence?

A Proceeds of Crime Act 2002

B Companies Act 2006

C Financial Services and Markets Act 2000

D Money Laundering Regulation 2007

14. Which of the following will generally not be an insider?

A A company director

B A market maker

C Someone who receives information from an insider

D A fund manager

15. Amanda is a retail investment adviser. She is assessing how close she is to meeting FCA requirements for Continuing Professional Development (CPD). In the year so far, she has carried out 28 hours of unstructured CPD and 16 hours of structured CPD. Which of the following further CPD hours must Amanda complete to meet the annual requirement?

A None, as she has already met the annual requirement

B 5 hours of structured CPD

C 5 hours of CPD which may be either structured or unstructured

D 12 hours of CPD of which 5 hours must be structured

16. **Which of the following is responsible for insider dealing legislation?**

   A   The Financial Service Authority

   B   The Department of Business, Innovation and Skills

   C   Her Majesty's Treasury

   D   The London Stock Exchange

17. **What is the maximum criminal sanction for assisting a money launderer?**

   A   14 years' imprisonment and a £1 million fine

   B   5 years' imprisonment and a £1 million fine

   C   14 years' imprisonment and an unlimited fine

   D   5 years' imprisonment and an unlimited fine

18. **Which of the following statements about insider dealing is false?**

   A   It only relates to unpublished, price-sensitive information

   B   Legislation covers unit trusts

   C   It is prosecuted by the FCA

   D   It cannot be prosecuted if information is passed on in the proper course of duties

19. **A market maker acting in good faith will not be prosecuted for insider dealing because there is**

   A   A special defence for market makers

   B   A general defence for market makers

   C   Defence covering bid facilitation

   D   Defence covering stabilisation

20. **Your bank has been approached by a senior member of an overseas government who is asking you to invest money on his behalf.**

   You suspect that the government may be funding itself through illegal seizure of assets belonging to its citizens and through illegal bribes.

   Which of these are important considerations when considering this investment from an ethical perspective?

   > I   Your bank's reputation
   >
   > II   Your bank's competitive advantage
   >
   > III   Money Laundering requirements
   >
   > IV   Your bank's profitability

   A   I, II, III and IV

   B   None of I, II, III and IV

   C   I and III only

   D   I, II and III only

21. An investor in an OEIC requests that the fund manager send her all reports about the progress of the fund that are required by the regulator. Which reports should she receive?

    A   A short report half-yearly and annually, and a long report half-yearly and annually

    B   A short report after the half-year end, and a long report annually

    C   A short report quarterly, and a long report half-yearly and annually

    D   A short report half-yearly and annually

22. By which of the following could inside information be supplied?

    I   A director of the company

    II   A secretary employed by the company

    III   A shareholder of the company

    A   I and II only

    B   I and III only

    C   II and III only

    D   I, II and III

23. All of the following are recognised as stages in the money laundering process, except

    A   The placement of cash into the financial system by opening a bank account

    B   Conducting a complex series of financial transactions to separate legitimate from illegitimate funds

    C   Undertaking illegal activities to generate funds to be laundered

    D   Purchasing income generating financial assets with previously invested illegal funds

24. Which of the following is the maximum penalty for the directors of an institution which fails to implement internal reporting procedures in respect of money laundering?

    A   Two years' imprisonment or an unlimited fine

    B   Five years' imprisonment and an unlimited fine

    C   Two years' imprisonment and an unlimited fine

    D   Six months' imprisonment and the statutory fine

Answers

1. **D** A professional client who is a large company is not an eligible claimant

   See Chapter 6 Section 10.2 of your Study Text

2. **B** A summary of complaints should be reported to the regulator every six months

   See Chapter 6 Section 8.8 of your Study Text

3. **B** Although the significant management controlled function extends to include proprietary traders who may exert significant influence on a firm, this will not cover all proprietary traders and 'proprietary trading function' is not a controlled function

   See Chapter 6 Section 1.3 of your Study Text

4. **D** The Financial Ombudsman Service is an alternative to the courts for an eligible complainant when a firm has failed to deal with a complaint to their satisfaction. The FOS maximum award is £150,000

   See Chapter 6 Section 9.2 of your Study Text

5. **D** An eligible complainant is someone who is a consumer; an enterprise with fewer than 10 employees and turnover or annual balance sheet not exceeding €2 million (called a micro-enterprise); a charity with annual income of less than £1 million; or a trust with a net asset value of less than £1 million

   See Chapter 6 Section 9.3 of your Study Text

6. **C** The firm is then bound by the Ombudsman's ruling

   See Chapter 6 Section 9.5 of your Study Text

7. **A** They must be given the FOS leaflet and told of their right to use the service

   See Chapter 6 Section 8.5 of your Study Text

8. **A** A firm must send to the complainant a prompt written acknowledgement providing 'early reassurance'

   See Chapter 6 Section 8.5 of your Study Text

9. **C** The complainant must first take his complaint to the firm. If it is not resolved to his satisfaction, he may go to the Financial Ombudsman Service

   See Chapter 6 Section 8.1 of your Study Text

10. **C** Authorised firms pay a levy towards the compensation scheme

    See Chapter 6 Section 10.1 of your Study Text

11. **D** This was increased to £85,000 to align with European standards

    See Chapter 6 Section 10.3 of your Study Text

12. **A** The FSCS is directly accountable to both the FCA and HMT

    See Chapter 6 Section 10.1 of your Study Text

13.   **A**   The Proceeds of Crime Act (POCA) 2002 supersedes the Criminal Justice Act (CJA) 1993

See Chapter 6 Section 4.6 of your Study Text

14.   **B**   As long as the dealing is in the course of normal market-making activities and the market maker acted in good faith, ie did not change their prices as a result of the information they were aware of

See Chapter 6 Section 5.1 of your Study Text

15.   **B**   Retail investment advisers must carry out at least 35 hours of CPD annually, of which 21 hours must be structured. If Amanda completes 5 hours of structured CPD, she will have met the requirement

See Chapter 6 Section 2.9 of your Study Text

16.   **C**   The legislation is the responsibility of Her Majesty's Treasury. Investigation and prosecution are the responsibility of the LSE and the FCA respectively

See Chapter 6 Section 5.1 of your Study Text

17.   **C**   The maximum penalty for the offence of assistance of a money launderer is 14 years' imprisonment and an unlimited fine, when found guilty in a Crown Court of law

See Chapter 6 Section 4.6.1 of your Study Text

18.   **B**   Unit trusts, in which there is no secondary market, are excluded from the legislation

See Chapter 6 Section 5 of your Study Text

19.   **A**   But only as long as they are acting in good faith; if not, they may be prosecuted

See Chapter 6 Section 5.5.1 of your Study Text

20.   **C**   Gaining a competitive advantage or making profits from doing business with money launderers is both unethical and illegal

See Chapter 6 Section 7 of your Study Text

21.   **A**   A short report and a long report must be prepared half-yearly and annually. The short report is to be sent to all unitholders, and the long report is to be made available to unitholders on request

See Chapter 6 Section 3.4 of your Study Text

22.   **D**   All employees are, by virtue of their office, potential holders of inside information. Shareholders are also a potential inside source

See Chapter 6 Section 5.2 of your Study Text

23.   **C**   The three stages in the money laundering process are placement, layering and integration. The criminal activity to get the funds in the first place is not included

See Chapter 6 Section 4.2 of your Study Text

24.   **C**   The maximum penalty would be a prison sentence together with a fine. Remember, liability does not require money laundering to have happened; simply not having the appropriate procedures in place is deemed to be serious enough

See Chapter 6 Section 4.5 of your Study Text

7. The Regulatory Advice Framework

Questions

1. When a discretionary manager buys and sells investments more than would be reasonably expected, given the client's agreed investment strategy, the rule that is potentially being breached is the rule related to

    A Best execution

    B Suitability

    C Churning

    D Burning

2. Appropriateness will need to be established

    A Before every transaction

    B For every class of investments and services at the outset of the business relationship

    C For non-advised sales

    D At the start of every business relationship

3. Which of the following would be a professional client?

    I   An entity requiring authorisation or regulation to operate in the financial markets

    II In relation to MiFID business, an undertaking with a balance sheet total of €25m, net turnover of €30m, and €1m own funds

    III In relation to MiFID business, as undertaking with a balance sheet of €20m, net turnover of €45m, and €1m own funds

    IV A non-MiFID business with share capital of £15m

    A I, II, III and IV

    B I, II and III only

    C I, III and IV only

    D II and IV only

4. None of the following are permissible goods and services in connection with the use of dealing commission arrangements, except

    A Portfolio valuation services

    B Travel and entertainment costs

    C Computer hardware associated with specialist software

    D Research providing original thought

5. **What can be sold to a client when making a cold call?**

    I   High volatility fund

    II   Life policy

    III   Unit trust based ISA

    IV   A FTSE 100 share where the customer relationship envisages such a call

    A   I, III and IV only

    B   II, III and IV only

    C   I, II and IV only

    D   II and III only

6. **Which of the following is not correct in respect of 'churning'?**

    A   It is prohibited by the best execution rule

    B   It involves an unsuitable series of transactions

    C   Its objective is to earn commission income

    D   It is not in the best interests of the consumer

7. **One of the categories into which clients may be allocated is 'eligible counterparty'. Which of the following rules will apply to the firm's relationship with eligible counterparties?**

    A   Client agreements

    B   Appropriateness

    C   Best execution

    D   Client categorisation

8. **A customer has asked you for clarification of the client money rules.**

    You explain that the main purpose of the rules is

    A   To protect customers against the effect of investments falling sharply in price

    B   To ensure that the highest level of interest on deposits accrues to customers

    C   To protect and segregate customer assets from those of the firm in case the firm gets into financial difficulties

    D   To protect the firm against claims of loss from customers

9. **In 2009, the financial services regulator published a consultation paper and proposals for implementing the Retail Distribution Review (RDR). The aims were to: improve the clarity with which firms describe their services to consumers; address the potential for adviser remuneration to distort consumer outcomes; and increase the professional standards of advisers. The RDR adviser charging regime does not apply to**

    A   Product providers who advise clients directly

    B   Advisers using pre-scripted questions to advise on stakeholder products

    C   Advisers giving independent advice on a full range of retail investment products

    D   Advisers giving advice on the products of a restricted range of product providers

10. **You are seeking to give investment advice on an independent basis, and you are expanding your awareness of the range of 'retail investment products'. Which of the following does not fall within the definition of retail investment products?**

    A   A self-invested personal pension plan

    B   A stakeholder pension plan

    C   Shares in an open ended investment company

    D   A deposit in a building society share account

11. **P & Q Investments have prepared a research report on a small pharmaceutical company. They are planning to make the report available to their clients.**

    Under which of the following circumstances is the firm allowed to deal ahead of releasing the research report?

    I   In anticipation of client orders

    II   When acting as a market maker

    III   When executing an unsolicited client trade

    A   I and II only

    B   I and III only

    C   II and III only

    D   I, II and III

12. **Your firm is conducting a review of its communications and has asked you to clarify the regulator's rules.**

    Under FCA rules, what is the status of an electronic communication?

    A   A firm may use electronic communications, but must follow it up with a formal paper communication

    B   It is the equivalent of communicating in writing

    C   It is not sufficient to only send an electronic communication

    D   The firm may insist on only communicating via electronic channels

13. **Gemma is considering an investment in an authorised UCITS funds but says that she would like to see a short document helping her to understand the nature and risks of the fund, to help with her decision to invest. Gemma should**

    A   Obtain a key investor information document, which the fund manager must prepare

    B   Ask whether the fund makes available a key investor information document, which is optional for the fund manager to prepare

    C   Obtain a prospectus, which the fund manager must prepare

    D   Ask whether the fund makes available a prospectus, which is optional for the fund manager to prepare

14. You have been asked to review the categorisations that have been allocated to the clients of your firm in respect of MiFID business.

    How would you categorise a company with €35m turnover, €18m balance sheet and €2.5m of own funds?

    A   *Per se* professional client

    B   *Per se* counterparty

    C   Retail client

    D   Elective professional client

15. Nazmi Kaya is a retail client of your firm. Nazmi requests in writing that he be treated as an elective professional client with respect to share purchases. Nazmi has worked for a major bank for nine months carrying out daily transactions in equity dealing, and has a portfolio worth £450,000.

    Which of the following best describes your firm's appropriate treatment of the client?

    A   As a retail client, as Nazmi does not satisfy the quantitative test for MiFID business

    B   As a retail client, as Nazmi does not satisfy the qualitative test

    C   As a *per se* professional client

    D   As an elective professional client

16. An FCA-regulated firm. Jeffreys & Sumter, issues an investment advertisement which invites readers to apply for units in a unit trust. A tear-off slip is provided.

    Which of the following criteria is the advertisement not required to meet?

    A   Be approved by the Financial Conduct Authority

    B   Be fair and not misleading

    C   Include details of charges or expenses

    D   Be tailored to the likely level of sophistication of the reader

17. An FCA-regulated firm, Fellowes Bryson Smythe, issues a financial promotion that is not a direct offer promotion.

    The firm must do all of the following, except which one?

    A   Apply appropriate expertise

    B   Ensure that the advertisement is clear, fair and not misleading

    C   Ensure that the advertisement identifies it as the issuer

    D   Ensure that the advertisement identifies it as regulated by the Financial Conduct Authority

18. **Which of the following is not exempt from financial promotions rules under s21 FSMA 2000?**

    A   Communications with certified high net worth individuals

    B   Promotions issued by a firm's appointed representatives

    C   Communications with overseas recipients

    D   Generic promotions

19. **Following a complaint, a firm concludes that Stephen, an investment adviser, should not have made a cold (unsolicited) call to Mr Singh.**

    This could be because

    A   The call was made following two unsuccessful attempts to call Mr Singh on the same day

    B   Stephen did not state the firm he worked for during the call

    C   The call was about a package product

    D   Mr Singh already has an established client relationship with the firm

20. **Harry Blunt, an independent financial adviser, is not required to supply a suitability letter. This is because**

    A   The client has been introduced to the IFA by another client

    B   The IFA is acting on a fee basis

    C   The business is conducted on an 'execution only' basis

    D   The IFA is regulated by the Financial Conduct Authority

21. **Rimcastle Investments is not required to assess appropriateness in respect of part of its business.**

    This is because the firm is executing client orders in

    A   Units in a collective investment scheme

    B   Derivatives

    C   Warrants

    D   Unlisted shares

22. **Barry has recently started a stakeholder pension plan. Barry is allowed a 'period of reflection' or 'cooling-off' period of**

    A   30 days

    B   21 days

    C   14 days

    D   7 days

23. **The following statements concern rules governing investment research activities. Which of the statements is false?**

    A Financial analysts can take positions in securities contrary to their current recommendations only in exceptional circumstances and with senior permission

    B Analysts must refrain from dealing on the information contained in research until the clients have been provided with time to consider it

    C Research analysts must not promise issuers favourable research coverage

    D The issuer should be permitted to review unpublished research on their company at any time

24. **Oakley & Sunderland makes a research recommendation. The firm must make disclosures in relation to all of the following, except**

    A All relationships and circumstances that may reasonably be expected to impair the objectivity of the recommendation

    B Whether employees involved have remuneration tied to investment banking transactions

    C Shareholding held by the issuer of over 3% of the share capital of the recommending firm

    D The names of those individuals involved in preparing the research

25. **Which of the following is true of the rule on inducements?**

    A The rule only applies to retail clients

    B Payments must be made by or on behalf of the client

    C Third party payments are allowed if immaterial and disclosed in the conflicts of interest policy

    D Third party payments are permitted if the client consents

26. **Which of the following is correct in respect of client money?**

    A IFA firms are not permitted to hold client money

    B An IFA firm may be authorised to handle client money and must hold such money in a designated client account

    C The client money rules are mainly designed to combat money laundering

    D An IFA firm may be authorised to handle client money and must hold such money in the firm's trading bank account

27. **A regulated firm leaves some of its own money in a client money account. This situation can be described as**

    A Pollution of client money account

    B Pollution of trust

    C Account in excess

    D Unreconciled account

Answers

1.   **C**   Churning involves dealing too frequently than is in the client's best interests

See Chapter 7 Section 7.8 of your Study Text

2.   **C**   Appropriateness rules apply where investment services are provided, other than making a personal recommendation and managing investments

See Chapter 7 Section 3.3 of your Study Text

3.   **C**   A large undertaking for MiFID business must have two of the following:
- – €20m balance sheet total
- – €40m net turnover
- – €2m own funds

See Chapter 7 Section 1.6.4 of your Study Text

4.   **D**   Only research and goods or services relating to the execution of trades are a permitted use of dealing commission

See Chapter 7 Section 7.5 of your Study Text

5.   **B**   The FTSE 100 share can only be sold if the relationship envisages the call

See Chapter 7 Section 2.13 of your Study Text

6.   **A**   A series of transactions that are each suitable when viewed in isolation may be unsuitable if the recommendation or the decisions to trade are made with a frequency that is not in the best interests of the client. The practice of 'churning' is not linked to the rule on best execution

See Chapter 7 Section 7.8 of your Study Text

7.   **D**   All other rules apply to retail and professional clients only

See Chapter 7 Section 1.2 of your Study Text

8.   **C**   The money segregated in client accounts should be covered by trust arrangements - for example, written confirmation from the bank that the firm is the legal owner but not the beneficial owner of the money in the client account

See Chapter 7 Section 6 of your Study Text

9.   **B**   The adviser charging rules do not apply to 'basic' pre-scripted advice on stakeholder products

See Chapter 7 Section 8.5.1 of your Study Text

10. **D**   The category of 'retail investment products' (RIPs) extends beyond the existing definition of packaged products to cover products in a packaged form that modifies the exposure to underlying assets compared with a direct holding of the financial asset. A building society deposit is not encompassed by the definition. Personal pension plans including SIPPs, stakeholder pension plans, and OEIC shares are all within the definition of RIPs

See Chapter 7 Section 8.3.2 of your Study Text

11. **C**   When research is provided to clients, the firm generally cannot act upon it until their clients have had the opportunity to act upon the research

See Chapter 7 Section 4.1 & 4.2 of your Study Text

12. **B**   The FCA's Handbook aims to be media-neutral, so that e-mail and other forms of electronic communications are given the same status as paper communications. Exclusive use of a website for electronic communications requires the consent of the customer

See Chapter 7 Section 1.4 of your Study Text

13. **A**   The fund manager must prepare both a prospectus and a KII document and, as a short document, the KII document is likely to better meet Gemma's requirements than the prospectus

See Chapter 7 Section 5.2.2 of your Study Text

14. **C**   A *per se* professional client must meet any two of the following criteria: balance sheet €20m, turnover €40m or own funds of €2m. This particular company only meets the own funds test and so must be categorised as a retail client

See Chapter 7 Section 1.6.4 of your Study Text

15. **A**   Although the client probably satisfies the qualitative test, we are unable to show that they satisfy two of the following criteria for the quantitative test

–   The client has carried out at least ten 'significant' transactions per quarter on the relevant market, over the last four quarters

–   The client's portfolio, including cash deposits, exceeds €500,000

–   The client has knowledge of the transactions envisaged from at least one year's professional work in the financial sector

We must therefore treat Nazmi as a retail client

See Chapter 7 Section 1.6 of your Study Text

16. **A**   Advertisements do not each need to be approved by the FCA, which would of course be quite an onerous task

See Chapter 7 Section 2 of your Study Text

17. **D**   The requirement to declare the FCA as the regulator only applies for direct offer financial promotions

See Chapter 7 Section 2 of your Study Text

18. **B**   A firm is required to apply the financial promotions rules to its appointed representatives

See Chapter 7 Section 2 of your Study Text

19. **B**   Cold/unsolicited calls are not allowed unless an existing customer envisages such a call, or the call relates to generally marketable packaged products, or it relates to a controlled activity/service regarding readily realisable securities. The adviser should identify himself and his firm, and should call 'at an appropriate time of day'. There is no rule specifically about calling after having made unsuccessful calls on the same day

See Chapter 7 Section 2.13 of your Study Text

20. C   A suitability letter is not supplied if the client is making the transaction on an 'execution only basis', as advice is then 'neither being sought nor given'

See Chapter 7 Section 3.2 of your Study Text

21. A   An appropriateness check is not required for certain non-complex financial instruments. Non-complex products include shares listed on a regulated market, money market instruments and units in a UCITS collective investment scheme. Complex products include warrants, derivatives and unlisted share

See Chapter 7 Section 3.3 of your Study Text

22. A   The maximum period of reflection is 30 days in this case

See Chapter 7 Section 5.3 of your Study Text

23. D   Pre-publication drafts can be previewed by the issuer only for the purpose of verifying compliance

See Chapter 7 Section 4 of your Study Text

24. C   The requirement to state the research firm's holding in the subject or vice versa starts at 5%

See Chapter 7 Section 4 of your Study Text

25. C   The rule on inducements applies to retail and professional clients. Inducements cover fees, commissions and non-monetary benefits paid to or by the client or someone on their behalf. Inducements are then only allowed if they do not impair compliance with the firm's duty to act in the best interests of the client and are generally disclosed in the conflicts of interest policy

See Chapter 7 Section 7.6 of your Study Text

26. B   Many small IFA firms are not authorised to hold client money but, if they are, it must be held in a designated client account

See Chapter 7 Section 6 of your Study Text

27. B   Client money should be segregated from firm's money

See Chapter 7 Section 6 of your Study Text

8. Principles and Outcomes Based Regulation

Questions

1. **Which of the following is not directly mentioned in the FCA's eleven Principles for Businesses?**

    A   Skill, care and diligence

    B   Relations with regulators

    C   Unreasonable charging

    D   Conflicts of interest

2. **To whom do the Principles for Businesses of the FCA apply?**

    A   All authorised firms

    B   All member firms of Designated Professional Bodies

    C   All Recognised Investment Exchange member firms

    D   All customers receiving financial advice

3. **Which of the following is not one of the Principles for Businesses of the FCA?**

    A   Clients' assets

    B   Integrity

    C   Polarisation

    D   Financial prudence

4. **One of the regulators' Principles for Businesses states: 'A firm must take reasonable care to ensure the suitability of its advice and discretionary decisions for any customer who is entitled to rely upon its judgement'. The Principle is**

    A   Principle 6: Customers' interests

    B   Principle 7: Communications with clients

    C   Principle 8: Conflicts of interest

    D   Principle 9: Customers: relationships of trust

5. **Which of the following is correct regarding the Statements of Principles for Approved Persons?**

    A   All apply to senior management only

    B   All apply to all approved persons

    C   Some apply to all approved persons and some apply to senior management only

    D   Some apply to all approved persons and some apply to those in customer functions only

6. **Which two of the following Statements of Principle apply to all approved persons?**

    A   Deal with the regulator in an open way; Skill, care and diligence in management

    B   Deal with the regulator in an open way; Integrity

    C   Skill, care and diligence in management; Integrity

    D   Deal with the regulator in an open way; Comply with regulatory requirements

7. **All of the following Statements of Principle apply only to persons carrying out controlled functions with significant influence, except which one?**

    A   Must comply with all of the regulatory requirements

    B   Due skill, care and diligence in management

    C   Observe proper standards of market conduct

    D   Business of the firm is organised and controlled effectively

8. **SYSC rules on apportionment of responsibilities relate to, and expand on, the Principle for Businesses of**

    A   Integrity

    B   Skill, care and diligence

    C   Management and control

    D   Communication with clients

9. **The principle of integrity is the first statement of principle for Approved Persons. The Code of Practice for Approved Persons (APER) includes various examples of behaviour which would be considered a breach of the statement of this principle. Which of the following would be least likely to be an example of such behaviour?**

    A   Providing false or inaccurate information to the regulator

    B   Deliberately aiming to achieve maximum appropriate profits

    C   Deliberately failing to disclose the existence of a conflict of interest

    D   Misleading others in the firm about the nature of risks being accepted

10. **There has been much discussion in recent years of different regulatory approaches in the financial services industry, and of the central concepts on which regulation is based.**

    Outcomes based regulation can be expected to have the result that

    A   Appropriate examination passes will be required for staff in a wider range of roles

    B   Customer confidence will increase and firms will experience increased business

    C   Continuing Professional Development will be given greater prominence

    D   Relatively more of firms' income will be generated from fees compared with commissions

11.   **The Statements of Principle 1 to 4 do not apply to**

    A   Employees of a firm who are not approved persons in respect of regulated activities generally

    B   Approved persons in respect of regulated activities that are not controlled functions

    C   Approved persons in respect of controlled functions

    D   Approved persons carrying out a significant-influence function

12.   **What is the main rationale for enabling the FCA to make product intervention rules that are temporary?**

    A   To limit the FCA's powers to shorter-term interventions

    B   To avoid imminent possible detriment to consumers

    C   As a low-cost solution that avoids costly consultations

    D   To deal with a systemic financial crisis

Answers

1.　**C**　Firms must treat customers 'fairly', but unreasonable charging is not mentioned

See Chapter 8 Section 1.2 of your Study Text

2.　**A**　The Principles for Businesses are for the protection of all customers and apply to all authorised firms

See Chapter 8 Section 1.3 of your Study Text

3.　**C**　Polarisation, which has been abolished during 2005, is not one of the eleven Principles for Businesses

See Chapter 8 Section 1.2 of your Study Text

4.　**D**　The Principle stated is Principle 9. Principle 6 states: 'A firm must pay due regard to the interests of its customers and treat them fairly'. Principle 7 states: 'A firm must pay due regard to the information needs of its clients, and communicate information to them in a way which is clear, fair and not misleading'. Principle 8 states: 'A firm must manage conflict of interest fairly, both between itself and its customers and between a customer and another client'

See Chapter 8 Section 1.2 of your Study Text

5.　**C**　Principles 1-4 apply to all approved persons. Principles 5-7 apply to senior management only

See Chapter 8 Section 3.2 of your Study Text

6.　**B**　Skill, Care and Diligence and Complying with Regulatory Requirements only apply to approved persons carrying out significant influence functions

See Chapter 8 Section 3.2 of your Study Text

7.　**C**　This question is asking which of the Statements of Principle apply to all types of controlled functions. Significant influence functions are those controlled functions that also have senior management responsibilities

See Chapter 8 Section 3.2 of your Study Text

8.　**C**　SYSC states that a firm must take reasonable care to establish and maintain appropriate systems and controls

See Chapter 8 Section 1.2 of your Study Text

9.　**B**　The list of examples is long and you would not be expected to learn each example. You should however be able to recognise behaviour in line with acting with integrity. In this question, aiming to maximise profits seems to be a normal business aim rather than a breach of integrity

See Chapter 8 Section 3.4 of your Study Text

10.　**B**　Outcomes-based regulation focuses on outcomes for consumers rather than the detail of rule compliance

See Chapter 8 Section 2.3 of your Study Text

11. **A** Note that, under the Financial Services Act 2012 (FSA 2012), the Statements of Principle relate not only to an individual's conduct in relation to the controlled functions they perform, but also to any other regulated activities functions they perform which relate to the firm within which they hold their approved person status. The Statements are not set out as covering those who are not approved persons, since they deal with the accountable functions of approved persons

See Chapter 8 Section 3 of your Study Text

12. **B** The power to make temporary rules, without the normal consultations, can be used if the FCA considers that the delay involved in complying with the requirement would be prejudicial to the interests of consumers

See Chapter 8 Section 4 of your Study Text

9. Ethical Behaviour and Professional Standards

Questions

1. **John Maple recently left his employer to start a new business. He did not sign a non-compete agreement with his old employer and is operating in the same industry. When he leaves, he contacts his old clients to tell them of his new business, using the telephone directory to obtain their telephone numbers. Which one of the following statements regarding John's conduct is most appropriate?**

   A John has breached Standard IV.A Loyalty by contacting his old clients

   B John has breached Standard V.B Communication with Clients and Prospective Clients by contacting clients using the phone book

   C John has breached both Standard IV.A Loyalty and Standard V.B Communication with Clients and Prospective Clients

   D John has not breached any Standards

2. **Diana Jones is an analyst working for ABC Investment Advisers. One of ABC's clients in the mergers and acquisitions department is XYZ Inc. and ABC's President is a director of XYZ. Diana has been asked to write a report on XYZ. Which one of the following courses of action is most appropriate?**

   A Do not write a report due to the directorship held by ABC's President

   B Write a report of a purely factual nature

   C Write a report but disclose in it the relationship between ABC and XYZ

   D Do not write the report if it would express a favourable opinion on XYZ

3. **Which one of the following is *least likely* to be a breach of Standard II.B – Market Manipulation?**

   A Spreading a rumour about the poor health of a company's CEO to depress its share price

   B Transacting in back-to-back buy/sell strategies in order to exploit tax loopholes

   C Issuing the price of a security by issuing a misleading statement

   D Building a dominant position in a commodity in order to influence the price of a related derivative

4. **Scott Blair is an analyst at Ice Investment Company. He is currently working closely with Volcano Inc, a chocolate company that is in the process of preparing for a secondary equity offering. Scott is taking part in a conference call with Volcano, who are discussing the failed launch of a new product. The failed launch will result in a significant drop in earnings. Throughout the call, members of the Ice sales team are wandering in and out of Scott's office and hear the information about the failed launch and earnings fall. As a result, they sell stock from client, proprietary and employee accounts. Which of the following statements is most appropriate?**

    A   Scott has breached Standard II.A Material Non-public Information by allowing the sales team in his office, but the sales team has not breached Standard II.A Material Non-public Information because they did not misappropriate the information

    B   Scott has not breached Standard II.A Material Non-public Information because he did not trade on the information or encourage the sales team to do so, but the sales team has breached Standard II.A Material Non-public Information by trading on the information

    C   Scott has not breached Standard II.A Material Non-public Information because he did not trade on the information or encourage the sales team to do so, and the sales team has not breached Standard II.A Material Non-public Information because they did not misappropriate the information

    D   Scott has breached Standard II.A Material Non-public Information because he did not prevent the transfer of the information and the sales team has breached Standard II.A Material Non-public Information by trading on the information

5. **The term 'material' in the phrase 'material nonpublic information' refers to information that is likely to significantly affect the market price of the issuing company's securities, or that is**

    A   Derived by the financial analyst from direct communication with an issuing company's management

    B   Likely to preclude the financial analyst or the analyst's firm from rendering unbiased or objective advice

    C   Acquired by the financial analyst from a special or confidential relationship with the issuing company

    D   Likely to be considered important by reasonable investors in determining whether to trade a particular security

6. **Jane Doe is a junior research analyst with Howard & Sons, a brokerage and investment banking firm. Howard's mergers and acquisitions department, which handles mergers and acquisitions, has represented Britland Company in all its acquisitions for the past 20 years. Two of Howard's senior officers are directors of various Britland subsidiaries. Doe has been asked to write a research report on Britland. In the context of the Code and Standards, what is Doe's best course of action?**

    A   Doe may write the report provided the officers agree not to alter it

    B   Doe may write the report if she discloses Howard & Sons' special relationship with Britland in the report

    C   Doe may write the report but must refrain from expressing any opinions because of the special relationships between the two companies

    D   Doe should not write the report because the two Howard & Sons officers are 'constructive insiders'

7. **Adam Long, an equity analyst, has got a one-off freelance assignment with Caspian, a fund management firm, whose CEO he knows from previous employment. The assignment is a report on Agala Inc, which was agreed over a meal and sealed with a handshake. Just before completing the task he is offered an interview for a full-time analyst position at a leading equity house. To impress them with the quality of his work, he is thinking of showing them the work he has done on Agala. Which of the following statements is most appropriate?**

   A   Adam cannot show the work he has done on Agala to his prospective employer as this would be a breach of Standard II.B – Market Manipulation

   B   Adam can show his work to his prospective employer because it is his work which he has not yet shown to Caspian and he has no written contract with Caspian

   C   Adam must disclose his work to his prospective employer as not to do so would be a breach of Standard VI.A – Disclosure of Conflicts, which requires disclosure of all matters of potential interest to potential employers

   D   Adam should not disclose his work even though he has no written contract with Caspian. To do so would be a likely breach of Standard IV.A – Loyalty

8. **Paula Yavy, a senior equity analyst at Hollander, has recently completed some research into Casco Inc and concluded that the stock should go on Hollander's buy list. Following well documented internal procedures she calls a team meeting and notifies her subordinates of her decision. One of her team, knowing it is against the firm's rules, buys stocks in Casco for their own account. Paula does not become aware of this action. Which of the following statements is most appropriate?**

   A   Paula has breached Standard VI.A – Responsibilities of Supervisors as she should not have allowed one of her team to trade the stock based on her buy recommendation

   B   Paula has not breached Standard VI.A – Responsibilities of Supervisors as she was following well documented procedures to prevent what happened from happening

   C   Paula has breached Standard VI.A – Responsibilities of Supervisors as she failed to supervise reasonably and adequately the actions of those she supervises

   D   Paula has not breached Standard VI.A – Responsibilities of Supervisors as even the best designed compliance procedures cannot prevent all breaches from occurring

9. **Fred Connor is a precious metals analyst for Alpha Securities and has just finished a report on Gamma Gold mining Inc. In the report he has included an estimate of the gold reserves of Gamma's mines. Connor arrived at his estimation based on sample drilling information released by the company. In his opinion, the company has large reserves. On the back of his estimation he has made a buy recommendation. Which of the following standards is most likely to have been breached?**

   A   Standard III.A – Loyalty, Prudence and Care

   B   Standard IV.C – Responsibilities of Supervisors

   C   Standard V.A – Diligence and Reasonable Basis

   D   Standard V.B – Communication with Clients and Prospective Clients

10. **Neil Smith is on a business trip to Japan to meet the management of one of the firms that he covers as a research analyst. He is currently rating the company as a 'buy'. While in a meeting, he is informed by the management that they are anticipating significant delivery problems at most of their factories and that this will have a negative impact on sales. No other analyst currently knows this information. Which of the following statements is most accurate?**

   A   Neil must change his recommendation to a sell, as to not include the information would breach his fiduciary duty to his clients

   B   Neil must not change his recommendation under any circumstances as to do so would breach the Code and Standards on the use of material nonpublic information

   C   Neil should encourage the company to disseminate the news to the market before publishing his own updated recommendation

   D   Neil must not issue a recommendation on the stock until the extent of the delivery problem is known

11. **Which one of the following is most likely to conflict with CFA Institute Code and Standards?**

   A   Analysts may change their investment recommendations without obtaining approval from their supervisor

   B   Personal account transactions by analysts should not be scrutinized for confidentiality reasons

   C   A portfolio manager should conduct a fact-find about a new customer before undertaking investment action on the customer's behalf

   D   A portfolio manager receives gifts from clients but discloses these to his employer

12. **Burt Hoffman is a portfolio manager who has the pension plan of a company as an account. The company's directors are asking him to vote in their favour at a forthcoming stakeholders' meeting. Since the account is a large one, Burt does not wish to offend the directors and risk losing it.**

   In addition, Burt puts the transactions of the account through a broker who gives Burt useful investment advice on European equities. This information is of no use in relation to the pension plan account but is useful for other accounts. The broker gives best execution and offers very low commissions.

   Burt reviews the arguments for and against the directors and decides that the balance of argument is in their favour and votes for them. Which of the following statements is most appropriate?

   A   Burt has violated CFA Standards by voting for the directors and by using the broker for the account's transactions

   B   Burt has violated CFA Standards by voting for the directors

   C   Burt has violated CFA Standards by using the broker for the account's transactions

   D   Burt has not violated CFA Standards

13. Which of the following is most appropriate with respect to Standard I.A – Knowledge of the Law for an analyst who is a CFA Institute member operating overseas, where the local laws are less strict than US laws and CFA Institute Code and Standards and where local laws apply?

A The analyst must follow US laws in conducting his investment activities, since he is a US citizen

B The analyst must follow local laws because they are less strict than US law and CFA Institute Code and Standards

C The analyst must follow the appropriate international laws, since there is a conflict between the level of severity of local and US laws and regulations

D The analyst must follow CFA Institute Code and Standards since they are stricter than the local laws

14. Matthew Brown has just completed a quantitative analysis of stock returns relative to book value for a number of stocks over the last year. Ben Evans has just overheard a conversation that a company is likely to be reporting higher earnings this year. Both now issue research reports on the basis of the above. Which one of the following statements is most appropriate?

A Both Matthew and Ben have breached Standards

B Neither has breached Standards

C Ben has breached Standards

D Matthew has breached Standards

15. Which of the following would not describe one of Jerome's duties as an agent?

A Exercising skill and care

B Delegating responsibilities

C Acting in good faith

D Obeying instructions

16. Lucy Miller is an analyst for the seafood industry. She has just received a package from the Lobster Shank, a company that is not one of her existing clients, containing 100 kilos of lobster tails – a delicacy. Miller estimates that the tails are worth over £6,000. According to the CFA Institute Code and Standards Lucy should

A Advise her superior of the gift and split it with him

B Accept the gift, since it is from a company rather than a client

C Refuse the gift because the Standards of Professional Conduct prohibit analysts from receiving gifts from the companies or industries they review

D Return the gift, as it is a large gift from a company

17. Jerome is told during his induction of the firm's emphasis on managerial responsibility for ethical behaviour combined with a concern for the law. This approach might best be described as being which of the following?

A Supervision approach

B An integrity-based programme

C A rules-based programme

D Professional enforcement

18. Pendleton Willard Asset Management have recently begun promoting a system of ethics qualities such as fairness, objectivity, charity, forethought, loyalty into their daily behaviour and decision-making. Which of the following would best describe the system of ethics being employed?

A Virtue ethics

B Deontology

C Compliance based ethics

D Utilitarianism

Answers

1. **D**   John can contact his old clients once he has left his old company provided he does not use his client lists to do so

   See Chapter 9 Section 1.3 of your Study Text

2. **C**   Standard VI.A – Disclosure of Conflicts

   See Chapter 9 Section 1.3 of your Study Text

3. **B**   Buying and selling securities for tax reasons, known as tax-loss harvesting, is allowed

   See Chapter 9 Section 1.3 of your Study Text

4. **D**   Standard II.A – Material Non-public Information

   See Chapter 9 Section 1.3 of your Study Text

5. **D**   Standard II.A – Material Non-public Information

   See Chapter 9 Section 1.3 of your Study Text

6. **B**   Standard VI.A – Disclosure of Conflicts

   See Chapter 9 Section 1.3 of your Study Text

7. **D**   Standard IV.A – Loyalty. Even though Adam has no written contract he has an obligation to let Caspian act on the work he has done and should not disclose it to a prospective employer unless he obtains permission from Caspian to do so

   See Chapter 9 Section 1.3 of your Study Text

8. **C**   Paula has failed in her supervisory role, not because her recommendation was acted upon as there were adequate procedures in place to prevent this, but because there were no procedures in place to review or record trading in a recommended stock

   See Chapter 9 Section 1.3 of your Study Text

9. **C**   Connor should base his recommendation on more information that a drilling estimate

   See Chapter 9 Section 1.3 of your Study Text

10. **C**   Standard II.A Material Non-public Information. Neil cannot trade or cause others to trade on the information unless it has been disseminated to the public

   See Chapter 9 Section 1.3 of your Study Text

11. **B**   Standard IV.C – Responsibilities of Supervisors. Checks should be carried out by supervisors

   See Chapter 9 Section 1.3 of your Study Text

12.   D   Standard III.A – Loyalty, Prudence and Care states that members 'have a duty of loyalty to their clients and must act with reasonable care and exercise prudent judgment'. They 'must act for the benefit of their clients and place their clients' interests before their employer's or their own interests'.   Burt has not violated the Standards. His vote for the directors is supported by his opinion on their arguments. His choice of broker is in the interests of clients because the broker offers best execution and low commissions

See Chapter 9 Section 1.3 of your Study Text

13.   D   The rule of thumb is to follow the stricter of applicable legal requirements and the Code and Standards

See Chapter 9 Section 1.3 of your Study Text

14.   A   Standard V.A – Diligence and Reasonable Basis. A longer period of analysis would be required for Matthew

See Chapter 9 Section 1.3 of your Study Text

15.   B   When acting as an agent, duties must not be delegated to someone else

See Chapter 9 Section 2.7 of your Study Text

16.   D   Standard I.B – Independence and Objectivity suggests modest gifts and entertainment are acceptable. Every member should avoid situations that might cause, or be perceived to cause, a loss of independence or objectivity in recommending investments or taking investment actions. Gifts from clients are less of a problem than gifts from a company

See Chapter 9 Section 1.3 of your Study Text

17.   B   An integrity-based approach combines a concern for the law with an emphasis on managerial responsibility for ethical behaviour

See Chapter 9 Section 2.11.2 of your Study Text

18.   A   The idea of virtue ethics is that if people cultivate certain values / principles or virtues / qualities, their behaviour is likely to be inherently ethical. Deontology refers to using duty as a label for the ethical approach

See Chapter 9 Section 2.10.4 of your Study Text

10. Client Objectives and Investment Advice

Questions

1.   **The liabilities of pension funds are predominantly**

   A   Long-term real liabilities

   B   Long-term fixed liabilities

   C   Short-term real liabilities

   D   Short-term fixed liabilities

2.   **Brian is 38 years old and owns a two-bedroom flat in Cambridge. He has a mortgage that is provided by a bank. The flat was new when Brian bought it ten years ago.**

   Gwenn is 49 years old and lives in a terraced house in Oxford. She has taken out two loans on the property. One was taken out to finance the purchase. The second mortgage was taken out to finance improvements which enhanced the value of the property.

   Over a recent period, both Brian and Gwenn have both seen their loan-to-value ratio fall.

   Which of the following statements is the most likely explanation of why Brian's loan-to-value ratio has, over the period in question, fallen less than Gwenn's loan to value ratio has fallen?

   A   House prices have risen more in Cambridge than Oxford

   B   House prices have risen in Cambridge but have fallen in Oxford

   C   House prices have risen more in Oxford than Cambridge

   D   House prices have risen in Oxford but have fallen in Cambridge

3.   **Which of the following is not a reason for the decline in defined benefit (DB) pension schemes and the rise of defined contribution (DC) schemes?**

   A   Higher liabilities in DB schemes

   B   Decreased longevity

   C   Falling returns on pension scheme assets

   D   Increasing pension deficits

4.   **The operation of a unit trust is generally regulated by**

   A   The Financial Conduct Authority

   B   The Bank of England

   C   The London Stock Exchange

   D   HM Treasury

5. **Which of the following best describes strategic asset allocation?**

A Strategic asset allocation is the practice of adjusting portfolio weights, when the portfolio manager believes that the relationship between asset classes will change during the near future

B Strategic asset allocation is the process of attempting to identify the intrinsic value of a share

C Strategic asset allocation is the process of allocating a portfolio among available assets in order to achieve the objectives of the portfolio

D Strategic asset allocation is the process attempting to exploit recurring and predictable share price movements

6. **Which of the following statements about life assurance funds is/are not true?**

I Any contributions paid into the life assurance fund are paid net of tax

II Capital gains within the fund are not taxable

III Any interest accumulated within the fund is not taxable

A I, II and III

B II only

C II and III only

D III only

7. **If a pension fund is said to be a mature pension fund, which of the following statements is this referring to?**

A The pension fund has invested in assets that are said to be mature assets due to the age of the asset being invested in

B The pension fund has individuals who contribute into the pension fund who are mature in age

C The pension fund has been in existence for longer than other similar funds in the same peer group

D The pension fund has invested in government-backed bonds which are near to maturity, when the redemption proceeds will be received in order to meet a particular liability

8. **Which of the following funds are more likely to purchase index-linked gilts?**

A Investment trust companies

B Authorised unit trusts

C Pension funds

D Life assurance companies

9. **Which of the following are likely to be liability-driven investors?**

I General insurance funds

II Someone saving for school fees

III Unit trusts

A I and II only

B I and III only

C II and III only

D I, II and III

10. **Which of the following is likely to be a return-maximising investor?**

   A   Pension fund

   B   ETF

   C   Investment trust

   D   General insurance fund

11. **Denby Shotover is an investment firm with a range of institutional clients, an asset management arm and a newly acquired private client business. Which of the following of the firm's clients is likely to have the most complex objectives?**

   A   A Venture Capital Trust

   B   A wealthy private client

   C   An Exchange Traded Fund

   D   A pension fund

12. **Which of the following are nominal liabilities?**

   I   Bank loan
   II   Future college fees
   III   Credit card liabilities

   A   I and II only

   B   I and III only

   C   II and III only

   D   I, II and III

13. **Which of the following are real liabilities?**

   I   School fees
   II   Personal pension
   III   Income provision for children

   A   I and II only

   B   I and III only

   C   II and III only

   D   I, II and III

14. **Which of the following are soft facts in a fact find?**

   A   Bank overdrafts

   B   Current investment holdings

   C   Client aspirations

   D   Current income

15. **What is the best description of shortfall risk?**

    A   Potential variability of inflation rates

    B   Potential variability of interest rates

    C   Potential variability of current fund values

    D   Potential variability of future fund values

16. **An independent financial adviser advised a client to transfer a personal pension contract to Provider A. One month later, the arrangement was transferred to Provider B. The adviser had received commission from Provider A, which was not clawed back, and also from Provider B. The client was not disadvantaged by the transfers.**

    The adviser's actions in this case are

    A   Ethical and compliant

    B   Ethical but not compliant

    C   Compliant but not ethical

    D   Neither ethical nor compliant

17. **When setting investment objectives for an investor's portfolio, the investor's tax status**

    A   Is irrelevant

    B   Can influence the investor's preference for income or capital and therefore dictate the composition of the portfolio

    C   Is only relevant for UK investors

    D   Will only affect investment decisions concerning equity

18. **Edward and Edwina Smith are in their mid-30s and are hoping to retire before they reach 60 and still be able to maintain their lifestyles. Neither of them has any pension arrangement. Which of the following will be the most important starting point for giving advice?**

    A   An analysis of household income

    B   An analysis of their existing life assurance policies

    C   Details of their children

    D   Details of their expense claims

19. **Your client, Bob, is in his mid-30s and has listed his financial objectives as follows.**

   - Retire age 60
   - Protect his family in the event of his death or ill health
   - Repay his mortgage within 10 years

   Having costed these options, you find that Bob has insufficient income to afford all of these objectives. What advice would you offer him?

   A That he can achieve all objectives

   B Regulations require a fully funded pension must take priority

   C His mortgage lender can determine his priorities

   D He must choose which objectives to prioritise

20. **Hanna is a retail client who works as a junior hospital doctor. She has little time to spend on organising her financial affairs. She now has saved money which she wishes to invest over the medium and long term.**

   What is the least important consideration if you recommend an investment in a collective investment scheme for Hanna?

   A Historical performance of the fund relative to peers

   B Management and other charges

   C Whether the fund is structured as a Unit Trust or an OEIC

   D Riskiness of the sector in which the fund is invested

Answers

1. **A** Long-term time horizon, with real liabilities affected by inflation

   See Chapter 10 Section 2.3 of your Study Text

2. **C** The equity a homeowner has in the home increases as the LTV ratio decreases. House price rises will tend to reduce the loan-to-value ratio of the borrower. House price falls will increase the homeowner's LTV, which is not the case for either Brian or Gwenn

   See Chapter 10 Section 1 of your Study Text

3. **B** Along with the other factors A, B and D, increased, and not decreased, longevity, is one of the reasons

   See Chapter 10 Section 3.2.3 of your Study Text

4. **A** The FCA regulates unit trusts

   See Chapter 10 Section 2.9.6 of your Study Text

5. **C** The strategic asset allocation is not fixed permanently, nor is it changed regularly. In the UK, it is common to review the strategic asset allocation once every three years

   See Chapter 10 Section 2.8 of your Study Text

6. **C** Life assurance funds have a different tax position than pension funds. The investment returns within a life assurance fund are subject to both income tax and capital gains tax. Also, any contributions paid into the fund by an investor will be paid out of their post-tax income

   See Chapter 10 Section 3.3 of your Study Text

7. **B** The maturity of a pension fund is with reference to the average age of the individuals who contribute into the pension fund. The two extremes would be a 'young' pension fund, where the pension fund has a longer time horizon, and a 'mature' pension fund, where the pension fund has a shorter time horizon to consider

   See Chapter 10 Section 2.6.3 of your Study Text

8. **C** Index-linked gilts are most likely to be purchased by pension funds, as they are trying to meet a 'real' liability in the future rather than a 'nominal' liability, and so an index-linked gilt that offers an inflation-protected, real return would be an ideal investment to buy

   See Chapter 10 Section 2.3 of your Study Text

9. **A** An unit trust will seek to maximise profits

   See Chapter 10 Section 2.2.4 of your Study Text

10. **C** An investment trust will seek to maximise profits, other funds aim to achieve matching (ETFs matching an index, not seeking outperformance)

    See Chapter 10 Section 2.2.4 of your Study Text

11. **B** A wealthy private client is likely to have several objectives to meet, perhaps with similar priorities. The funds will each have one primary objective

See Chapter 10 Section 2.2.4 of your Study Text

12. **B** Future college fees represent a real liability

See Chapter 10 Section 2.3 of your Study Text

13. **D** All are real liabilities

See Chapter 10 Section 2.3 of your Study Text

14. **C** Client aspirations are subjective, being incapable of objective quantification

See Chapter 10 Section 2.5 of your Study Text

15. **D** The risks described are, respectively, inflation risk, interest rate risk, capital risk, shortfall risk

See Chapter 10 Section 2.6.1 of your Study Text

16. **C** Provider B has borne the loss of the commission payment, but the client has not lost out

See Chapter 10 Section 1 of your Study Text

17. **B** Capital gains can be advantageous for tax purposes

See Chapter 10 Section 2.5 of your Study Text

18. **A** Affordability will be the primary concern, hence household income is the most important

See Chapter 10 Section 2.2 of your Study Text

19. **D** An individual's financial priorities are for him to determine

See Chapter 10 Section 2.3 of your Study Text

20. **C** The technical differences between OEICs and unit trusts are less important than the other reasons quoted

See Chapter 10 Section 1 of your Study Text

11. The UK Tax System

Questions

1. A UK company makes profits before tax of £120,000 in the financial year 2012, including gross dividend income from other companies of £30,000. What is the company's tax liability for the year, to the nearest pound?

   Important! You should enter only the answer in numbers (without spaces, letters or symbols) strictly using the following format: 00000

2. The 20% rate of corporation tax applies to companies which earn profits plus gross dividends of

   A Less than £1,500,000

   B Between £150,000 and £300,000

   C Below £10,000

   D Less than £300,000

3. Which of the following is not tax-free income for an individual?

   A Interest on gilts

   B Proceeds of a qualifying life assurance policy

   C Income from an ISA

   D Interest on National Savings Certificates

4. Which of the following is true in relation to income tax on salary?

   A The personal allowance is £8,105 and the basic rate of tax 20%

   B The personal allowance is £8,105 and the basic rate of tax 10%

   C The personal allowance is £10,600 and the basic rate of tax 18%

   D The personal allowance is £10,600 and the basic rate of tax 32.5%

5. An individual has made two chargeable disposals in the year. The chargeable gains have been calculated as £12,800 and £3,900 and neither is eligible for entrepreneurs' relief. There are also brought forward losses of £2,000. If the individual has taxable income of £33,970, what would be the capital gains tax for the year (in £), if the annual exempt amount is £10,600?

   Important! You should enter only the answer in numbers (without spaces, letters or symbols) strictly using the following format: 0000

6. What is the CGT annual exempt amount for an individual for 2012/13?

   A £7,475

   B £8,105

   C £10,600

   D £11,280

7. Presuming that tax on dividends is paid at the higher rate of 32.5%, for someone with 10,000 shares upon which net dividend of 16p per share is paid, what additional tax should be paid, to the nearest pound?

   Important! You should enter only the answer in numbers (without spaces, letters or symbols) strictly using the following format: 000

   ┌─────────────────────────────┐
   │   │
   └─────────────────────────────┘

8. An individual disposes of shares in company A for £60,700 and company B for £30,000, having purchased them for £48,000 and £32,000 respectively. If income tax is paid at the higher rate, the exempt amount is £10,600 and entrepreneurs' relief is not available, what CGT is payable?

   A £28

   B £110

   C £140

   D Nil

9. Sally buys a property, not in a disadvantaged area, for £650,000. How much stamp duty land tax must she pay?

   A £6,500

   B £14,750

   C £19,500

   D £26,000

10. If a higher rate taxpayer pays £1,000 additional tax following receipt of a dividend, the notional tax credit being 10%, then what was the net dividend received by the taxpayer, to the nearest pound?

    Important! You should enter only the answer in numbers (without spaces, letters or symbols) strictly using the following format: 0000

    ┌─────────────────────────────┐
    │   │
    └─────────────────────────────┘

11. **From which of the following sources is free of income tax?**

       I   NS&I Savings Certificates

       II   3½% War Loan

       III   NS&I Direct Saver Account

       IV   Individual Savings Accounts

A I, II, III and IV

B I, II and IV only

C I and IV only

D None of I, II, III and IV

12. **Which of the following are not chargeable to capital gains tax?**

       I   Sale of gilts

       II   Sale of Eurobonds

       III   Sale of convertible debt denominated in sterling

A I, II and III

B I and II only

C I and III only

D I only

13. **It is 1 May and an investor receives a dividend of £56.82. What is the amount of the tax credit attached?**

A £5.00

B £6.31

C £14.20

D £11.36

14. **Kevin makes a gift of £175,000 to a trust on 9 July 2012. He had previously made gross chargeable transfers of £145,000 in January 2004 and £173,000 in May 2007. The trustees agree to pay the lifetime tax. How much do they have to pay on the gift made in July 2012, to the nearest pound?**

Important! You should enter only the answer in numbers (without spaces, letters or symbols) strictly using the following format: format: 0000

15. **What is the highest rate of tax that discretionary trusts may be required to pay on their dividend income?**

A 10%

B 32.5%

C 42.5%

D 50%

16. **What is the standard rate of VAT?**

   A 0%

   B 5%

   C 17.5%

   D 20%

17. **At what rate is Stamp Duty Reserve Tax charged?**

   A 0.5%

   B 1%

   C 3%

   D 4%

18. **On which dates are the payments on account for 2012/13 due?**

     I   31 January 2012

     II   31 January 2013

     III   31 July 2012

     IV   31 July 2013

   A I and III only

   B II and IV only

   C I, II and III only

   D II, III and IV only

Answers

1. **18000**

	£	
Augmented profits	120,000	
	(30,000)	
Total profits	90,000	@ 20% = £18,000

    The company has augmented profits (ie, profits including gross dividend income) of less than £300,000: therefore we use the small profits rate

    See Chapter 11 Section 7 of your Study Text

2. **D**   The small profits rate

    See Chapter 11 Section 7.3 of your Study Text

3. **A**   Gilt interest is paid gross (unless an election for 20% withholding tax is made), but is still liable to income tax

    See Chapter 11 Section 1.2.2 of your Study Text

4. **A**   20% is the basic rate of income tax for salaries and interest income. £10,600 is the capital gains tax annual exempt amount

    See Chapter 11 Sections 1.3.2 and 1.3.3 of your Study Text

5. **1108**

	£
Chargeable gains	16,700
Less: loss brought forward	(2,000)
Less: annual exemption	(10,600)
	4,100

    As entrepreneurs' relief is not applicable on either gain, the entire gain is taxable. Since the investor has other taxable income of £33,970 (£400 below the higher rate threshold) the tax payable is calculated as

    18% × £400 + 28% × £3,700 = £72 + £1,036 = £1,108

    See Chapter 11 Section 3 of your Study Text

6. **C**   The CGT annual exempt amount is £10,600

    See Chapter 11 Section 3.3.2 of your Study Text

7. **400**   The gross dividend is $10,000 \times 16p \times \frac{100}{90} = £1,778$

    The extra tax is the difference between 32.5% and 10% on this amount

    £1,778 × 22.5% = £400

    See Chapter 11 Section 1.3.5 of your Study Text

8. **A** (£60,700 – £48,000) + (£30,000 – £32,000) – £10,600 = £100

   Since the investor is a higher rate tax payer, the rate should be 28%

   Applying the tax rate of 28% gives a CGT of £100 × 28% = £28

   Note that in this case you are given the annual exemption amount. Tax rates and allowances change and you are likely to be given this information in the exam

   See Chapter 11 Section 3 of your Study Text

9. **D** £26,000 (£650,000 × 4%)

   See Chapter 11 Section 6.1.2 of your Study Text

10. **4000** Investor pays the difference between 10% and 32½% of the gross dividend, £1,000

   Therefore gross dividend = $\dfrac{£1,000}{0.225}$ = £4,444.44

   Therefore net dividend = £4,444.44 × 90% = £4,000

   or

   £1,000 = 25% of net div

   Therefore, £1,000 = 0.25 × £x

   £ = $\dfrac{£1,000}{0.25}$ = £4,000

   See Chapter 11 Section 1.3.5 of your Study Text

11. **C** National Savings & Investments Savings Certificates and Individual Savings Accounts pay income free of UK Income and Capital Gains Tax

   See Chapter 11 Section 1.2.2 of your Study Text

12. **D** Capital gains on Eurobonds and convertible bonds are subject to capital gains tax

   See Chapter 11 Section 3.1.3 of your Study Text

13. **B** This amount is received net of a notional 10% income tax. To calculate the original amount, we need to multiply by 100/90. This gives a gross dividend of £63.13 meaning that the tax credit was the difference, ie £6.31 (or simply divide the net dividend by 9)

   See Chapter 11 Section 1.3.5 of your Study Text

14. **3400** Transfer of value 9 July 2012

	£	£
Cash gift		175,000
Less: AE 2012/13		(3,000)
AE 2011/12 b/f		(3,000)
Gross transfer of value		169,000
Nil rate band at gift	325,000	
Less: GCTs in 7 years before gift	(173,000)	
Nil rate band remaining		(152,000)
Taxable		17,000
Tax @ 20%		3,400

   See Chapter 11 Section 4.6 of your Study Text

15. **C** The dividend trust rate is 42.5%

    See Chapter 11 Section 4.8.4 of your Study Text

16. **D** The standard VAT rate is 20%, the reduced rate (eg, for domestic fuel) is at 5%

    See Chapter 11 Section 8.2 of your Study Text

17. **A** 0.5%

    See Chapter 11 Section 6.2.2 of your Study Text

18. **B** Due on 31 January in the tax year and 31 July after the tax year ends

    See Chapter 11 Section 5.2.3 of your Study Text

12. The Taxation of Investments

Questions

1. **Which of the following best describes the amount that an individual may pay into their pension with tax relief in 2012/2013?**

    A   The higher of £3,600 and their earnings in the tax year, subject to a cap of £50,000

    B   The lower of £3,600 and their earnings in the tax year

    C   The higher of £3,600 and their earnings in the tax year, subject to a cap of £150,000

    D   £3,600 for non-taxpayers and £50,000 for taxpayers

2. **For the tax year 2012/2013, what is the maximum sum, in £, that anyone can invest in an ISA?**

    Important! You should enter only the answer in numbers (without spaces, letters or symbols) strictly using the following format: 00000

3. **Which of the following is not true of REITs?**

    A   They are listed companies

    B   They may elect for their property income to be exempt from corporation tax

    C   It is not possible to hold a REIT with an ISA

    D   Disposals of REIT shares may be subject to CGT

4. **The Junior ISA is best described as**

    A   A way to take advantage of Government payments and tax relief on investments for a child born after 2 January 2011

    B   A way for a child born before 3 January 2011 and holding a Child Trust Fund to continue to receive Government payments and tax relief on investments

    C   A scheme of tax-free investment for or on behalf of a child in which £3,600 can be invested annually

    D   A scheme of tax-free investment for or on behalf of a child in which £1,000 can be invested annually

5. **An investor sells shares that he purchased 10 years ago. Which of the following statements regarding tax allowances on the sale are correct?**

    A   The investor will receive a CGT exemption allowance only

    B   The investor will receive no CGT exemption allowance nor any other allowance

    C   The investor will receive a CGT exemption allowance only and an allowance for inflation

    D   The investor will receive a CGT exemption allowance and an allowance related to the period the shares were held

6. Which of the following would incur a CGT liability on sale?

A   Private car

B   Gilts

C   Currency used in a trading account

D   Shares in an ISA wrapper

Use the following information to answer Question 7 to 10

Bill Swinson is a higher rate taxpayer with a salary of £85,000 per year. He also received £7,200 net in coupon interest from an investment in bonds as well as dividends of £6,480 from his investments in shares.

7. How much (to the nearest £) is Bill's personal allowance for income tax purposes?

Important! You should enter only the answer in numbers (without spaces, letters or symbols) strictly using the following format: 0000

---

8. How much extra tax (to the nearest £) is Bill liable to pay in respect of the bond coupon interest?

Important! You should enter only the answer in numbers (without spaces, letters or symbols) strictly using the following format: 0000

---

9. How much further tax is Bill liable to pay in respect of his dividend income?

Important! You should enter only the answer in numbers (without spaces, letters or symbols) strictly using the following format: 0000

---

10. What was Bill's total tax liability (including taxes deducted at source) for the year in question, to the nearest £?

Important! You should enter only the answer in numbers (without spaces, letters or symbols) strictly using the following format: 00000

Answers

1.   **A**   Payments are capped at £50,000 and A is currently the best answer given

     See Chapter 12 Section 2.1.3 of your Study Text

2.   **11280**   Up to £5,640 may be invested in cash deposits

     See Chapter 12 Section 2.3.4 of your Study Text

3.   **C**   REITs can be held in an ISA

     See Chapter 12 Section 2.7 of your Study Text

4.   **C**   There will be no Government payments for Junior ISA holders. £3,600 can be invested annually

     See Chapter 12 Section 2.4 of your Study Text

5.   **A**   Investors receive an annual allowance on capital gains, only

     See Chapter 12 Section 1.4.2 of your Study Text

6.   **C**   Gilts do not incur CGT liability and any assets in an Individual Savings Account are free of any tax. A car is generally considered a wasting asset which incurs no CGT. However currency gains made via a trading account would be subject to CGT

     See Chapter 12 Section 1 and 2 of your Study Text

7.   **7505**   Bill's earned income is £85,000. We are told that he received £7,200 net in coupon interest, implying that 20% had already been deducted from gross interest of £9,000 (= £7,200 / 0.8). Bill received £6,480 in dividend income: this would be after deducting 10% tax therefore, implying that the gross dividend was £7,200 (= £6,480 / 0.9). Total income = £85,000 + £9,000 + £7,200 = £101,200. This exceeds £100,000 by £1,200, thus reducing the standard personal allowance of £8,105 by £1,200 / 2 = £600. Thus, Bill's personal allowance is £7,505

     See Chapter 12 Section 1 of your Study Text

8.   **1800**   Since Bill is a higher rate taxpayer, he will pay at a rate of 40% on the bond interest. He received £7,200 net in coupon interest, giving gross interest of £9,000 (= £7,200 / 0.8). Therefore, he will need to pay a further 20% of £9,000 which equals £1,800

     See Chapter 12 Section 1 of your Study Text

9.   **1620**   £6,480 in dividend income is after the deduction of 10% tax, giving a gross dividend of £7,200 (= £6,480 / 0.9). Since higher rate tax on dividends is 32.5%, Joe must pay an extra 22.5% on the gross dividend, which equals £1,620

     See Chapter 12 Section 1 of your Study Text

10. 30064 The answer is calculated in the following Table. Note that the question asks for the total tax liability, and not the total tax due.

	Earnings £	Interest £	Dividends £
Total earnings	85,000		
Interest £7,200 × 100/80		9,000	
Dividends £6,480 × 100/90			7,200
Less: personal allowance (£600 reduction)	(7,505)		
Taxable income	77,495	9,000	7,200

	£
Tax on first £34,370 @ 20%	6,874
Tax on next £43,125 @ 40%	17,250
Tax on £9,000 @ 40%	3,600
Tax on £7,200 @ 32.5%	2,340
Total tax liability	30,064
Less: tax deducted at source	
On dividends: £7,200 × 10%	(720)
On interest: £9,000 × 20%	(1,800)
Total tax due	27,544

See Chapter 12 Section 1 of your Study Text

13. Tax Planning

Questions

1. **Which of the following would be least appropriate as a method of reducing CGT liability?**

    A   Transferring the ownership of assets to a spouse or civil partner

    B   Dispose of EIS shares

    C   Selling any exempt assets that they own simply to achieve a tax free return

    D   Realise gains within the annual exempt amount, so that there is no actual taxable gain

2. **Which of the following is least likely to be recommended as a tax-efficient investment?**

    A   Personal Pension Plan

    B   Individual Savings Account

    C   High Interest Savings Account

    D   Enterprise Investment Scheme

3. **Where an investor owns a rental property which provides income of £17,000 per year and then transfers 50% ownership of the property to their husband who has no other income, how much income tax liability will the husband have, to the nearest pound, after the transfer?**

    Important! You should enter only the answer in numbers (without spaces, letters or symbols) strictly using the following format: 00

    [   ]

4. **What is the maximum gross sum that a parent may pay into a child's building society savings account gross before the income becomes treated as income from the parent and taxed as such? The account is not a Junior ISA, a cash ISA, nor a Child Trust Fund.**

    Important! You should enter only the answer in numbers (without spaces, letters or symbols) strictly using the following format: 000

    [   ]

5. **Which of the following would be treated as a gift with reservation (GWR) for IHT purposes?**

    A   Giving away a holiday cottage but continuing to spend long holidays there paying a market rent

    B   Giving away a house but continuing to live in it at a below market rent

    C   Giving away a painting

    D   Creating a trust which you do not benefit from

6. Florence Devere died on 1 November 2012 leaving £162,500 to her surviving spouse Kevin and the remaining £195,000 of her estate to her only child. The IHT nil rate band for 2012/13 is £325,000. Which of the following is correct?

   A On his death, Kevin's estate cannot take advantage of any transfer of Florence's nil rate band

   B On his death, Kevin's estate can take advantage of 40% additional nil rate band as a result of Florence's nil rate band being transferred

   C On his death, Kevin's estate can take advantage of 50% additional nil rate band as a result of Florence's nil rate band being transferred

   D On his death, Kevin's estate can take advantage of 60% additional nil rate band as a result of Florence's nil rate band being transferred

---

Use the following information to answer Questions 7 to 10

Ashley and Cheryl, a married couple, have asked you to provide them with investment advice. During the fact find process you have determined their existing investments, set out in the table below. All the investments are presently in Ashley's name.

Ashley has taxable income of £58,000 and Cheryl has taxable income of £8,500. The annual CGT exemption is £10,600.

Type of asset	Current Value	Purchase price
Gilts	£18,500	£12,000
Shares in Big Boots plc	£16,000	£20,000
Vintage wine	£30,000	£9,000
Bank savings account	£25,000	£22,000
Buy to let flat	£400,000	£250,000

Give your answers to the nearest pound.

7. What would be the CGT liability if the vintage wine was sold?

   Important! You should enter only the answer in numbers (without spaces, letters or symbols) strictly using the following format: 0000

   ```
   
   ```

---

8. What would be the total CGT liability if the shares in Big Boots Plc were sold at the same time as the vintage wine?

   Important! You should enter only the answer in numbers (without spaces, letters or symbols) strictly using the following format: 0000

   ```
   
   ```

9. What would be the CGT liability if the wine was sold after being fully transferred into Cheryl's name?

    Important! You should enter only the answer in numbers (without spaces, letters or symbols) strictly using the following format: 0000

    [   ]

10. How much CGT is saved by transferring the wine into Cheryl's name before selling?

    Important! You should enter only the answer in numbers (without spaces, letters or symbols) strictly using the following format: 0000

    [   ]

Answers

1. **C** A little tricky but we are advised that the tax tail should not wag the dog and so selling assets simply because they are tax-exempt would not be advisable

    See Chapter 13 Section 2.2 of your Study Text

2. **C** While the other investments all offer tax reductions, there is no such reduction for an ordinary savings account that is not within a tax wrapper, and the interest will be charged to income tax

    See Chapter 13 Section 1.4 of your Study Text

3. **79** Each will be taxed as though they own 50% of the property as joint owners. The husband's liability will therefore be £8,500 – £8,105 @ 20% = £79

    See Chapter 13 Section 1.2.2 of your Study Text

4. **100** Note that this only applies to parents and not grandparents

    See Chapter 13 Section 1.3 of your Study Text

5. **B** Gifts with reservation occur when an individual gifts property and continues to enjoy the benefit of the asset, either rent free or at reduced cost, or the person getting the gift does so with conditions attached

    See Chapter 13 Section 3.3.2 of your Study Text

6. **B** The transfer to Kevin is exempt from IHT. The remaining transfer to the child amounts to 60% of Florence's nil rate band, leaving 40% to transfer to Kevin, the surviving spouse

    See Chapter 13 Section 3.2.2 of your Study Text

7. **2912** The gain is £21,000 (= 30,000 – 9,000). The first £10,600 is subject to the annual CGT exemption. The taxable gain is £10,400 at 28%, as Ashley is higher rate tax payer

    See Chapter 13 Section 2 of your Study Text

8. **1792** The total gain is £17,000 (= (16,000 + 30,000) – (20,000 + 9,000)), as the loss on the shares partially offsets the gain on the wine. The first £10,600 is exempt from CGT, leaving a taxable gain of £6,400, taxable at the higher rate of 28% = £1,792

    See Chapter 13 Section 2 of your Study Text

9. **1872** Taxable gain of £10,400, taxed at basic CGT rate of 18% = £1,872

    See Chapter 13 Section 2 of your Study Text

10. **1040** £2,912 CGT incurred at higher rate less £1,872 at lower rate

    See Chapter 13 Section 2 of your Study Text

Practice Examinations

Contents

	Page Number	
	Questions	**Answers**
Practice Examination 1	95	113
Practice Examination 2	121	139
Practice Examination 3	147	165
Practice Examination 4	173	191
Practice Examination 5	199	217

The Unit 1 The Investment Environment examination consists of 85 questions, to be answered in 1 hour and 40 minutes. There will be a small number of additional questions which will not be marked as these are new questions included for evaluation purposes. Your examination is therefore based on 85 marked questions, although you will not be informed which are marked and which are not.

Most of the questions will be four-part multiple choice questions but the exam will also contain a number of gap-fill questions for numerical areas. With a gap-fill question, no selection of possible answers is offered: you must enter your answer in the space provided.

The five practice examinations presented here each has 85 questions (the number that are marked in the examination) and you should allow yourself a time limit of 1 hour and 40 minutes for each exam.

PRACTICE EXAMINATION 1

(85 questions in 1 hour and 40 minutes)

1. Which of the following is not one of the objectives of the Financial Conduct Authority, as provided in FSMA 2000?

    A Securing an appropriate degree of protection for consumers

    B Ensuring that the relevant markets function well

    C Ensuring stable prices and confidence in the currency

    D Promoting effective competition in the market for regulated financial services

2. What is the standard settlement term on shares traded through the London Stock Exchange?

    A T+1

    B T+2

    C T+3

    D T+5

3. Which of the following is not true with regard to asset allocation?

    A It is designed to achieve better risk/return outcomes than from just investing in one asset class

    B It is the last stage of the investment management process

    C It would include consideration of investing in cash

    D It is influenced by a client's objectives and constraints

4. How would you describe the risks of investing in cash?

    A Capital risk

    B Interest rate risk

    C Capital and interest rate risk

    D Neither capital nor interest rate risk

5. What is the main reason why a pension fund would hold equities?

    A To immunise the portfolio

    B To hedge the inflation risk in the liabilities

    C Because the fund manager believes that the return will match the fund's future liabilities

    D To match the risk profile of the fund's liabilities

6. **What is the amount of tax, in pounds and pence, that has been withheld on a dividend where the amount paid out to the shareholder was 50p?**

   Important! You should enter only the answer in numbers (without spaces, letters or symbols) strictly using the following format: 0.00

   ┌─────────────────────────────┐
   │   │
   │   │
   └─────────────────────────────┘

7. **What is the last stage of the process of investing a retail client's funds?**

   A Asset allocation

   B Fact find

   C Fund selection

   D Market timing

8. **Against which of the following company's annual profits can this year's losses be offset for corporation tax purposes?**

   I   Profits of this year

   II   Future year's gains from the same trade

   III Last year's profits

   A I and II only

   B I and III only

   C II and III only

   D I, II and III

9. **Who is the main clearing body for trades carried out over the Tokyo Stock Exchange?**

   A Japanese Securities Clearing Corporation

   B Euronext

   C Clearstream

   D DTCC

10. **How are Japanese Government Bonds traded?**

    A Over the counter

    B Tokyo Stock Exchange

    C Osaka Stock Exchange

    D Through the Japanese Government

11. In the context of company meetings, which of the following are correct with regards to proxies?

   I   The proxy must be able to vote in two ways on each issue

   II The proxy form must state that the member gives consent for the proxy to vote on their behalf

   III The proxy form must state in which direction the proxy must vote

   A II only

   B I and II only

   C I and III only

   D I, II and III

12. Under the CFA Institute Code and Principles, which of the following is most accurate with regard to an employee leaving their current firm and joining a rival?

   A The employee may take information with regards to the current clients of their existing firm

   B The employee may take a valuation model which was developed at the firm where they currently work for which the employee was involved in the development of

   C The employee may take partly complete research reports which the employee was working on before leaving their current firm

   D The employee may take knowledge gained from attending a training course whilst employed at their current firm

13. Under the CFA Code and Principles, which of the following would be most likely to be considered market manipulation?

   A Buying shares in a company after having recommended to clients to buy the same company's shares

   B Selling share in a company after having recommended to clients to sell the shares in the same company

   C Buying shares in a company on behalf of clients to push the share price up before selling personal holdings of shares

   D Buying shares in a company before buying shares on behalf of your clients

14. Which pair of words most closely describe a 'financial promotion'?

   A Advertisement / encouragement

   B Incentive / publicity

   C Invitation / inducement

   D Prospectus / upgrade

15. Under the CFA Code and Principles, if an adviser is about to recommend buying shares which the adviser holds herself, what is the most appropriate action to be taken?

   A The adviser should sell her own shares before making the recommendation

   B The adviser should not make the recommendation since she owns shares herself

   C The adviser should disclose to her clients that she owns shares themselves

   D The adviser is not required to do anything with regards to making this recommendation

16. **With whom is a lasting power of attorney required to be registered?**

    A   The Crown Court

    B   The Attorney Agency

    C   The Ministry of Justice

    D   The Office of the Public Guardian

17. **Which of the following are covered by the FCA's Principles for Businesses?**

    I   Protection of client assets

    II   Communication of relevant information to clients

    III   Skill, care and diligence

    A   II and III only

    B   I and II only

    C   I and III only

    D   I, II and III

18. **The FCA suspects that a new computer system implemented by Sweetwater & Cranley, an authorised firm, will be insufficient to deal with the trading volume of the business and will most likely lead to inefficient execution of client trades. In this case**

    A   The firm can be punished because a principle has been broken

    B   The firm can be punished because a principle will be broken

    C   The firm cannot be punished because a principle has not been broken yet

    D   The firm cannot be punished because a principle will not be broken

19. **Which of the following promotions would not be covered by the financial promotions order rules?**

    A   A direct offer financial promotion to a retail client

    B   An offer to a group of business angels to buy 50% of the shares of a company

    C   An email to all of a firm's existing clients with regards to a new product they are offering

    D   An advert on a billboard relating to a firm's existing product range

20. **Which of the following would be considered by the FCA in relation to a firm's application for authorisation?**

    I   The firm's business model

    II   The applicant's fitness and propriety

    III   Close links that the applicant has to other firms

    A   II only

    B   I and II only

    C   I and III only

    D   I, II and III

21. **How can Dubois Carhaix, a French investment firm, who wishes to open up a branch in the UK, obtain the necessary regulatory approval?**

    A   Apply for a waiver from the FCA

    B   Apply for Part 4A permission from the FCA

    C   Apply to the French regulator for authorisation

    D   Passport into the UK via MiFID

22. **Under the CFA Code and Standards, which of the following statements is correct with regard to a new investment fund? The fund has created a simulated portfolio of how they would have traded over the last three years.**

    A   The performance of the simulated portfolio cannot be included in any promotional material because it is only simulated

    B   The performance of the simulated portfolio cannot be included in any promotional material since it only covers three years

    C   The performance of the simulated portfolio can be included so long as it is clearly disclosed that the performance was not actually achieved

    D   There are no additional disclose requirements

23. **The FCA believes that an adviser has been purchasing and selling shares too frequently within a client's portfolio. This practice is an example of**

    A   Churning

    B   Aggregation

    C   Switching

    D   Front running

24. **The maximum jail sentence for assisting a money launderer is**

    A   2 years

    B   5 years

    C   7 years

    D   14 years

25. **Which of the following could potentially generate a capital gains tax liability on disposal?**

    A   Government bonds

    B   An individual's main home

    C   Antique jewellery

    D   Car

26. **Which of the following is correct with regards to a fact find?**

    A The fact find must be completed prior to any meeting between the investment adviser and the client

    B The fact find has to be documented and kept up to date on an annual basis

    C All factual data must be verified before the provision of any investment advice

    D There are no specific regulatory requirements with regard to a fact find

27. **Mr Dunwoody has a number of financial objectives, among which, in descending order of priority, are to be mortgage-free, to be able to send his only child to private school, and to be able to take three foreign holidays a year.**

    Mr Dunwoody currently owes £12,000 in credit card debt, on which he pays an APR of 15.5%. Which of the following is most likely to be what you would advise Mr Dunwoody to do with some surplus cash savings which he has?

    A Reduce his credit card debt

    B Take out a larger life assurance policy

    C Repay some of the principal on the loan he used to buy his current home

    D Invest in zero coupon bonds which mature when his child is ready to start private school

28. **International accounting standards require derivatives to be valued on the company's balance sheet at**

    A Cost

    B Amortised cost

    C Fair value

    D Market value

29. **Variation margin is best described as**

    A The maximum probable one day loss on the current open positions

    B A good faith deposit to demonstrate to the clearing house that you can pay your losses

    C The amount of money required to be paid into a margin account to cover the previous day's losses

    D The amount of money that can be taken out of a margin account represented by the previous day's trading gains

30. **The person who gains from the performance of the assets held in a discretionary trust is**

    A The settler

    B The trustee

    C The beneficiary

    D The remainderman

31. **Which of the following is a financial intermediary?**

　　　I　　An investment trust company

　　　II　　A building society

　　　III　　A defined benefit pension scheme

　　A　I only

　　B　II only

　　C　I and II only

　　D　I, II and III

32. **How should an authorised firm initially categorise a client that is a trust with assets of £1,000,000 and income of £10,000?**

　　A　Eligible counterparty

　　B　Professional client

　　C　Retail client

　　D　Authorised client

33. **Which of the following must apply for a firm to be able to reclassify a retail client to a professional client?**

　　　I　　The client must complete and pass a written assessment of their investment knowledge

　　　II　　The firm must have warned the client about protections lost by becoming a professional client

　　　III　　The client must confirm that they want to be classified as a professional client despite the protections lost

　　A　II and III only

　　B　I and II only

　　C　I and III only

　　D　I, II and III

34. **Which of the following is required with regard to a prospectus for a rights issue by a listed company?**

　　　I　　The prospectus must be made public

　　　II　　The prospectus must be approved by the UKLA

　　　III　　The prospectus must be approved by the LSE

　　A　I and II only

　　B　I and III only

　　C　II and III only

　　D　I, II and III

35. **A firm wishing to engage in stock lending of a client's assets**

    A   Is not obliged to inform the client that it is engaging in stock lending using the client's assets

    B   Must make only a general disclosure to clients that it may engage in stock lending using clients' assets

    C   Must obtain specific prior consent from the client to lend their stock

    D   Is not allowed to do so unless the client is an eligible counterparty

36. **Victoria has passed an appropriate examination which permits her to give advice on retail investment products, and another appropriate examination which permits her to give advice on regulated mortgage contracts. She does not hold any further appropriate examinations passes. In which of the following client transactions is Victoria not qualified to give advice?**

    A   A personal pension plan

    B   A home reversion plan

    C   A re-mortgage

    D   A unit-linked whole of life policy

37. **The rate of tax payable by a higher rate tax payer on dividend income is**

    A   10%

    B   25%

    C   32.5%

    D   42.5%

38. **Jane Dickson has an estate of £520,000 on her death. Calculate her inheritance tax liability to the nearest £, assuming 50% of her husband's inheritance tax nil rate band was unused when he died 5 years ago. The current level of the nil rate band is £325,000.**

    Important! You should enter only the answer in numbers (without spaces, letters or symbols) strictly using the following format: 00000

39. **Mr Singh is a widower who has assets of £375,000. He has one daughter. If he transfers ownership of all his assets to his daughter today, what is the minimum amount of inheritance tax that will have to be paid on this transfer?**

    A   £50,000

    B   £20,000

    C   £10,000

    D   Nil

40. **Mr and Mrs Renwick plan to transfer ownership of their home to their three children. What rules may have the result that this transfer has no inheritance tax advantage?**

   A   Benefit in interest rules

   B   Gifts with reservation rules

   C   Chargeable lifetime transfer rules

   D   Potentially exempt transfer rules

41. **Nigel Thwaite and Lucy Reese have lived together for six years. They may get married in the future, but have no plans to do so soon.**

   In addition to inheritance tax, what tax should Nigel consider when he transfers ownership of assets to Lucy?

   A   Value Added Tax

   B   National Insurance Contributions

   C   Income Tax

   D   Capital Gains Tax

42. **Mr and Mrs Kumar have assets of £455,000 and £555,000 respectively. How much inheritance tax will be payable in total, in pounds, if each of them dies when the nil rate band is £325,000 on the dates of each death?**

   Important! You should enter only the answer in numbers (without spaces, letters or symbols) strictly using the following format: 000000

   ```
   
   ```

43. **Julio prefers to invest in equities and Maria prefers to invest in gilts. What can be deduced about their attitudes towards risk?**

   A   Julio is more risk-tolerant than Maria

   B   Maria is more risk-tolerant than Julio

   C   Julio and Maria are both equally risk-tolerant

   D   Maria is more a risk-taker than Julio

44. **An investment adviser holds an initial meeting with a new client in which the adviser obtains information from the client about their salary, investment objectives and attitudes towards risk. What is the name of the document in which this information would be recorded?**

   A   Fact find

   B   Client summary

   C   Power of attorney

   D   Investment mandate

45. **Which of the following would be classified as a hard fact?**

    I   Details of salary

    II   Attitude towards risk

    III Desire to repay mortgage within the next ten years

    IV   Current value of outstanding mortgage balance

    A   I, II and III only

    B   I, II and IV only

    C   II and III only

    D   I and IV only

46. **German equities traded on the Deutsche Börse settle on**

    A   Euroclear

    B   Clearstream

    C   Eurex

    D   LCH.Clearnet

47. **What stamp duty land tax rate may apply on the granting of a residential lease?**

    A   1% of the sum of all the future lease payments

    B   1% of the present value of all the future lease payments

    C   5% of the sum of all the future lease payments

    D   5% of the present value of all the future lease payments

48. **Ainsley Peacock is a MiFID firm that is subject to CASS. How long after deciding to no longer use an institution for client money should the firm keep the records relating to this decision?**

    A   1 year

    B   3 years

    C   5 years

    D   7 years

49. **The least important consideration when recommending a collective investment scheme for a retail client is**

    A   Historical performance relative to peers

    B   Management and other charges

    C   Whether the fund is structured as a Unit Trust or an OEIC

    D   Riskiness of the sector in which the fund invests

50. Your role is that of a Financial Adviser at Renfrew, a company that has set an objective of growing its advisory business by 25% each year for the next three years.

You have completed a client fact find and you have prepared a statement of recommendations for the client. The client has indicated that she does not have much time to consider personal financial matters because of her demanding role as a Senior Graphic Designer with a nationally known advertising agency. When you explain your recommendations to the client, she has her pen ready in order to sign the necessary forms and does not ask any questions. You have the impression that she wants to keep the meeting as short as possible.

What is the most appropriate action you should take in this situation?

A   Ask the client questions to check that she has understood your recommendations before asking her to sign

B   Advise the client that you do not think it appropriate to proceed and suggest that she seek advice elsewhere

C   Given the firm's objective of growing the business, consult with your compliance officer before proceeding

D   Give the client the opportunity to sign as soon as you have explained your recommendations

51. Which of the following is correct in respect of French BTANs?

    I   They pay a gross coupon annually

    II   They are issued by Dutch auction

    III   They settle T+2 in the secondary market

A   I only

B   I and II only

C   II and III only

D   I, II and III

52. In which of the following circumstances must a director report her own transactions in shares of the company of which she is director?

A   Any purchase or sale of shares

B   Any purchase only of shares

C   Any purchase or sale that takes his holding above 3% of the company's issued share capital

D   Any purchase or sale only in a takeover situation

53. A team supervisor at Peawhite Investments is conducting a discussion of the Bribery Act 2010 (BA 2010) with his team. During the discussion, team members mention various statements that they have heard about the new Act. Which of the following statements by team members is least correct?

A Arnie mentions that firms will be subject to BA 2010 only if they have a 'demonstrable business presence' in the UK

B Colin states that guidance for firms on adequate procedures to prevent bribery has been issued by the Ministry of Justice

C Thea states that the Financial Conduct Authority is responsible for enforcing the criminal offences in BA 2010 for authorised firms

D Gemma says that firms can be prosecuted for failing to prevent bribery, if a person associated with it bribes another person on its behalf

54. At a barbecue party, Mitra overhears Miranda complaining that her husband is always home late because he is CEO of a company that has just been approached with a hostile takeover bid. The next day Mitra buys share for herself and for her clients. According to the CFA Institute's Standards of Practice, which of the following is correct?

A Mitra has not breached the standards because she heard the information in an non-work context

B Mitra has breached the standards because she bought shares for herself as well as her clients. She should only have traded for her clients

C Mitra has breached the standards because she traded on the basis of non-public information

D Mitra has breached the standards because she failed to make the information public

55. An analyst is compiling a research report. Which of the following is correct according to the CFA Institute Standards of Practice?

A She can use quotations from well-known economists without attributing them

B She can use spreadsheet models without referencing the source as long as she does her own analysis

C She can use excerpts from journals if the source is quoted

D She can reproduce the work of other analysts without reference to them as long as she is consistent with their conclusions

56. Kim is a basic rate tax payer and her husband Rupert is a higher rate tax payer. They both own gilts, within and outside their ISAs. Which of the following is the least tax-efficient action?

A Rupert transfers his gilts outside of the ISA to Kim

B Rupert transfers his gilts from inside the ISA to outside his ISA

C Kim transfers her gilts outside the ISA to Rupert

D Kim transfers her gilts from inside her ISA to outside her ISA

57. A pension fund's Statement of Investment Principles is the responsibility of

   A The actuary
   B The trustees
   C The investment advisers
   D The auditors

58. Bruce is concerned that his current investments will not enable him to pay off his interest only mortgage which matures in 15 years.

   Which asset class would be most appropriate for him to invest in if he wants the best chance of sufficient growth to pay off the mortgage?

   A Bank deposit account
   B Gilt-edged securities
   C Equities unit trust
   D Corporate bond fund

59. What is the name of the risk that an investor is exposed to if they are concerned that the value of their investment will not grow to a suitable amount to meet the liability?

   A Shortfall risk
   B Capital risk
   C Inflation risk
   D Sovereign risk

60. Life insurance companies often have a significant amount of their assets invested in long-term bonds. This is because long-term bonds

   A Are expected to generate a higher return than other asset classes
   B Have more exposure to interest rate risk
   C Provide matching cashflows for annuity liabilities
   D Provide real returns

61. Caitlin is an IFA who sometimes receives requests for advice beyond her area of expertise. She passes these requests from her clients on to a larger firm and receives a referral fee in return. According to the CFA Institute Standards of Practice

   A This arrangement is not acceptable due to the inherent conflict of interest
   B Caitlin can receive referral fees without disclosure as she could not have performed the work herself
   C Caitlin cannot receive referral fees unless the arrangement is once-only
   D Caitlin can receive the referral fees as long as disclosure is made to her clients

62. Arnold Schwartz and Christian Merriweather live together as civil partners. They currently live in a rented flat in Dorset, England. The landlord has agreed to sell the freehold to Arnold and Christian for £325,000. Arnold and Christian will be paying £45,000 towards the purchase cost and are seeking a repayment mortgage to fund the remainder of the purchase. What is the best way of establishing affordability of the mortgage for Arnold and Christian?

A Reviewing the last three months' payslips of Arnold and Christian

B Performing an analysis of monthly household income and outgoings

C Reviewing the current assets and liabilities of Arnold and Christian

D Undertaking an analysis of the risk profiles of Arnold and Christian

63. At what percentage of voting rights held by one shareholder would a listed company be required to make an announcement?

Important! You should enter only the answer in numbers (without spaces, letters or symbols) strictly using the following format: 0.0

┌─────────────────────┐
│   │
│   │
└─────────────────────┘

64. A man dies leaving half of his £499,200 estate to his children and the rest to his wife when the inheritance nil-rate band is £312,000. Three years later his wife dies leaving a total estate of £695,000 to their children when the nil-rate band is £325,000. How much inheritance tax will be payable, in £?

Important! You should enter only the answer in numbers (without spaces, letters or symbols) strictly using the following format: 000000

┌─────────────────────┐
│   │
│   │
└─────────────────────┘

The following information relates to questions 65 to 67

Barlow & Barlow (B&B) is a firm of financial advisers offering services to a wide variety of clients including large firms, investment banks and small individual private investors. They primarily offer research and advice into specialist areas including the pharmaceutical sector, but also offer more general financial advice. B&B's largest client is Jump plc, with whom they carry out non-MiFID business. Jump plc has a balance sheet total of €15,000,000 and 150 full time employees. Last year Jump plc had a turnover of €20,000,000.

65. Based on the information available, what would be the most appropriate client categorisation for Jump plc?

A Private client

B Retail client

C Per se professional client

D Per se eligible counterparty

66. Patrick is a retail client of B&B with a portfolio worth £450,000 who requests in writing that he be treated as an elective professional client with respect to share purchases. Patrick has worked for a major bank for nine months carrying out daily transactions in equity dealing. B&B should treat Patrick

   A   As a retail client for the reason that he does not satisfy the quantitative test for MiFID business
   B   As a retail client for the reason that he does not satisfy the qualitative test
   C   As a per se professional client
   D   As an elective professional client

67. When doing business with one of its clients, B&B provided the client with a basic agreement. The business involved arranging for the client to opt out of their work pension scheme and into a private scheme, four years ago. For how long does B&B need to keep a record of this agreement?

   A   2 years
   B   5 years
   C   7 years
   D   Indefinitely

68. COBS rules require communications with clients about designated investment business to meet a number of key criteria. Which of the following is not explicitly stated as one of these criteria?

   A   Not misleading
   B   Clear
   C   Comprehensive
   D   Fair

69. When communicating with clients to satisfy rules stating that the communication be in durable form, which of the following would be considered acceptable?

   I   Email
   II   Written letter
   III   USB storage device
   IV   Compact disc

   A   II only
   B   I and II only
   C   None of I, II III and IV
   D   I, II, III and IV

70. A broker firm F does business with an IFA firm which is doing this business on the instruction of an individual. Which of the following is true?

   A   The IFA firm is a client of F, unless there is an agreement with F to treat the individual as its client
   B   Both the IFA firm and the individual are clients of F
   C   The individual is an indirect customer of the broker, and this relationship cannot be altered
   D   The individual is a client of F, unless there is an agreement to the contrary

71. **What is the standard settlement term for Gilts traded through the London Stock Exchange?**

    A   T + 1

    B   T + 2

    C   T + 3

    D   T + 5

72. **Which is the dominant asset class in UK pension funds?**

    A   Bonds

    B   Equity

    C   Cash

    D   Antiques

73. **A client has a complaint against an authorised firm. To whom should the complaint be addressed initially?**

    A   The FCA

    B   The Financial Ombudsman

    C   The Competition Commission

    D   The authorised firm

74. **With respect to a defined benefit pension fund, who is responsible for preparing the Statement of Funding Principles?**

    A   The depositary

    B   The investment manager

    C   The plan sponsor

    D   The trustee

75. **Which of the following is not a MiFID core service or activity?**

    A   Advising on investment

    B   Discretionary management

    C   Dealing as principal

    D   Providing safeguarding services

76. **An investor owns 633 shares that each pay a net dividend of 12p. What is the total amount of the notional tax credit, in pounds and pence?**

    Important! You should enter only the answer in numbers (without spaces, letters or symbols) strictly using the following format: 0.00

77.   The three stages of money laundering are Placement, Layering and Integration. In which stages could an investment manager typically be used?

        I   Placement

        II   Layering

        III   Integration

A   I and II only

B   I and III only

C   II and III only

D   I, II and III

78.   In the context of authorisation by the FCA, which of the following is an exempt person?

A   An appointed representative

B   A private client adviser

C   A broker/dealer

D   A market maker

79.   The European Union (EU) has 27 member states. The main objective of the EU in financial services is

A   The facilitation of efficient financial services provision by ensuring the free movement of capital within the EU

B   The creation of a pan-European consumer protection agency to enforce the regulatory regimes of member States

C   The creation of a market in which authorised investment firms authorised in member States can engage in financial services business throughout the EU

D   The establishment of a single pan-European regulator with a single authorisation regime for financial services firms across the EU

80.   How long will the Competition Commission have initially to reach a decision about a takeover?

A   Three months

B   Four months

C   24 weeks

D   There is no stipulated time frame

81.   Which of the following can be a defence against a charge of insider dealing?

A   I only sold to prevent a loss

B   Other investors who did not have the information acted in a similar way

C   I believed the information to be widely known

D   I only bought shares for my clients

82. **With respect to money laundering, on whose advice do the FCA and Treasury place particular emphasis?**

   A   The Securities and Exchange Commission

   B   The Joint Money Laundering Steering Group

   C   The Financial Ombudsman Service

   D   The Financial Skills Partnership

83. **Which of the following is true with respect to the suitability rule?**

   I   The rule applies to retail clients only

   II   The rule applies when advising clients

   III   The rule applies when conducting discretionary management

   A   I and II only

   B   I and III only

   C   II and III only

   D   I, II and III

84. **How often should a firm report to the FCA with reference to complaints received?**

   A   Every month

   B   Quarterly

   C   Twice a year

   D   Annually

85. **ABC Investments have prepared a research report which they are planning to make available to their clients. Under which of the following circumstances can the firm deal ahead of releasing the research report?**

   I   In anticipation of client orders

   II   When acting as a market maker

   III   When executing an unsolicited client trade

   A   I and II only

   B   I and III only

   C   II and III only

   D   I, II and III

Answers

1. **C** Ensuring stable prices and confidence in the currency is part of the task of the Bank of England, in its core purpose of monetary stability. B is the FCA's single strategic objective. A and D are operational objectives of the FCA

   See Chapter 5 Section 1.3 of your Study Text

2. **C** The settlement period for equities traded through the London Stock Exchange is 3 business days after the trade date, or T+3

   See Chapter 2 Section 8.1 of your Study Text

3. **B** The last stage of the investment management process is stock or fund selection

   See Chapter 10 Section 2.7 of your Study Text

4. **B** When investing in cash there is no capital risk, as the value of the cash investment is not at risk, however a cash investment will typically be subject to interest rate risk, so as interest rates fall, less interest will be earned on the cash deposit

   See Chapter 10 Section 2.6 of your Study Text

5. **C** The investments made by a pension fund manager are all made with the aim of matching the liabilities of the pension fund and, as such, if the fund manager has invested in equity, then it will be because they believe this will help them to achieve the aim of matching the fund's liabilities

   See Chapter 10 Section 3.2 of your Study Text

6. **5.56** Dividends are paid net of 10% tax, so if a dividend has been paid of 50p, this is after 10% tax has been deducted. The gross (pre-tax) dividend can be calculated by dividing the net dividend by (1 – tax rate) or 0.9 (= 1 – 0.1). This gives a pre-tax dividend of 55.56p (= 50p / 0.9). 5.56p of tax has notionally been deducted before the dividend is paid

   See Chapter 12 Section 1.4.1 of your Study Text

7. **C** Fund selection is the last stage of the investment process

   See Chapter 10 Section 2.12 of your Study Text

8. **D** The year's losses can be offset against this year's profits, last year's profits and future profits of the same trade

   See Chapter 11 Section 7.4 of your Study Text

9. **A** The JSCC clears trades carried out over the Tokyo Stock Exchange

   See Chapter 2 Section 7.4.1 of your Study Text

10. **A** Japanese Government Bonds are traded OTC

    See Chapter 2 Section 7.4.2 of your Study Text

11. **A** A proxy can be either in the form whereby the proxy decides on the best way to vote in a resolution, or to be able to only vote in one particular way

    See Chapter 2 Section 5.8.5 of your Study Text

12. **D** An employee is not permitted to take anything with them when they leave a firm which is considered the property of the firm. The knowledge that the employee has is not the property of the firm

See Chapter 9 Section 1 of your Study Text

13. **C** In this set of transactions, the clients' holding has been purchased with the sole purpose of pushing the share price up. This is considered market manipulation

See Chapter 9 Section 1 of your Study Text

14. **C** The FCA's own description uses the words 'invitation' and 'inducement'

See Chapter 7 Section 2.1 of your Study Text

15. **C** The adviser can make this recommendation so long as their shareholding is disclosed to allow the clients to place the advice of the adviser its correct context

See Chapter 9 Section 1 of your Study Text

16. **D** A lasting power of attorney must be registered with the Office of the Public Guardian

See Chapter 3 Section 1.7 of your Study Text

17. **D** All of these points are covered by the FCA's Principles for Businesses

See Chapter 8 Section 1 of your Study Text

18. **A** Principles have already been breached: those of skill, care and diligence and management and control. This is because the firm has not put an appropriate dealing system in place

See Chapter 8 Section 1 of your Study Text

19. **B** A financial promotion made to sophisticated investors (which includes business angels) is not covered by the financial promotions order rules

See Chapter 7 Section 2.8 of your Study Text

20. **D** Within the threshold conditions are suitability, business model and effective supervision (including close links), so all of these factors would be considered in an application of authorisation

See Chapter 5 Section 3.3 of your Study Text

21. **D** A French firm conducting investment business would be able to open up a branch in the UK under the passporting arrangement contained within MiFID

See Chapter 1 Section 5.3 of your Study Text

22. **C** A simulated (or hypothetical) portfolio's performance can be included if clients are made aware that this is simulated performance and was not actually achieved

See Chapter 9 Section 1 of your Study Text

23. **A** When a firm is trading too frequently within a client's account, to no benefit for the clients, this is referred to as churning

See Chapter 7 Section 7.8 of your Study Text

24. **D** The maximum jail sentence for assisting a money launderer is 14 years

See Chapter 6 Section 4.6.1 of your Study Text

25. **C** A capital gains tax liability will not be created on the disposal of the principal primary residence, on gilts, nor on a wasting asset such as a car

See Chapter 11 Section 3.1.3 of your Study Text

26. **D** There are no specific legal or regulatory requirements with regards to the completion of a fact find

See Chapter 10 Section 2.5 of your Study Text

27. **A** The client's primary investment objective is to be mortgage-free, but – given the high APR on his credit card borrowing – it makes more sense to reduce the credit card balance than to repay some of the outstanding mortgage balance or make other investments

See Chapter 10 Section 2 of your Study Text

28. **C** IAS 39 requires that derivatives are recognised at their fair value

See Chapter 2 Section 6 of your Study Text

29. **C** Variation margin is additional margin that must be paid to cover the previous day's trading losses

See Chapter 2 Section 3.2 of your Study Text

30. **C** The beneficiary gains for the assets held in a discretionary trust

See Chapter 3 Section 6.3 of your Study Text

31. **D** All of these are considered financial intermediaries

See Chapter 1 Section 1.3 of your Study Text

32. **C** Trusts are treated as retail clients

See Chapter 7 Section 1.6 of your Study Text

33. **A** In addition, the firm must have assessed whether the client is eligible to be classified as a professional client, and the client must have requested the change in writing

See Chapter 7 Section 1.6.4 of your Study Text

34. **D** The prospectus must be approved by both the UKLA and the LSE, as well as being made available to the public

See Chapter 2 Section 4 of your Study Text

35. **C** A firm cannot engage in stock lending using a client's assets unless that client has given prior consent for their assets to be used in this way

See Chapter 7 Section 6 of your Study Text

36. **B** B will require an equity release qualification. The other options will be covered by retail investment products and mortgage advice qualifications

See Chapter 6 Section 2.6 of your Study Text

37. **C** The rate of tax payable by a higher rate tax payer on dividend income is 32.5%. Since 10% tax is deducted at source, the tax payer is required to pay an additional 25% of the dividend received to get to the total 32.5% rate

See Chapter 11 Section 1.3.5 of your Study Text

38. **13000** Jane can make use of her own nil rate band and also the unused proportion of her husband's nil rate band, making a total of £487,500 (£325,000 x 1.5). Once this is deducted from the total value of Jane's estate of £520,000 this leaves £32,500 subject to inheritance tax. The inheritance tax rate is 40%, meaning the IHT liability will be £13,000

   See Chapter 13 Section 3.2 of your Study Text

39. **D** If Mr Singh survives seven years from the date of the transfer, there will be no inheritance tax to pay

   See Chapter 11 Section 4 of your Study Text

40. **B** The gifts with reservation rules mean that if a transfer of the legal ownership of an asset takes place, but the original owner still retains some rights with regards to that asset (for example, living in a house rent-free) then, for the purposes of inheritance tax, the transfer will have been deemed to have not taken place

   See Chapter 13 Section 3.3 of your Study Text

41. **D** From the point of view of capital gains tax, this transfer will be treated as a chargeable disposal and so may generate a capital gains tax liability

   See Chapter 13 Section 2 of your Study Text

42. **144000**   Total value of estates: £1,010,000

   Total nil rate bands (transferable between spouses): £650,000

   Total estate subject to IHT: £360,000

   Total IHT payable (@40%): £144,000

   See Chapter 11 Section 4 of your Study Text

43. **A** Equities are riskier than gilts. Since Julio prefers investing in the more risky equities asset class, he is more tolerant of risk than Maria

   See Chapter 10 Section 2.6 of your Study Text

44. **A** Information gathered from a client should be documented in a fact find

   See Chapter 10 Section 2.5 of your Study Text

45. **D** Salary details and the outstanding balance on a mortgage are two examples of hard facts

   See Chapter 10 Section 2.5 of your Study Text

46. **B** Clearing, settlement and custody take place through Clearstream

   See Chapter 2 Section 7.6.1 of your Study Text

47. **B** The tax is only applied to leases where the present value is above £125,000, but this is the best answer available

   See Chapter 11 Section 6.1 of your Study Text

48. **C** The records should be retained for five years

   See Chapter 7 Section 6 of your Study Text

49. **C** The technical differences between OEIC and Unit trust are less important than the other reasons quoted

See Chapter 10 Section 4 of your Study Text

50. **A** It is important to ensure that the client has understood what you have said, even though she seems to want the meeting to be as short as possible. The firm's objective to grow its business is not relevant to the action you should take, as you should act in the client's best interests

See Chapter 9 Section 2 of your Study Text

51. **B** BTANs settle T+1 in the secondary market

See Chapter 2 Section 7.1 of your Study Text

52. **A** Disclosure rules require that all transactions are reported

See Chapter 2 Section 5.1 of your Study Text

53. **C** The regulator is not responsible for enforcement under BA 2010. Where the FCA finds evidence of criminal matters, it will refer them to the Serious Fraud Office, who are the UK lead agency for criminal prosecutions for corruption. However, authorised firms who fail to address corruption and bribery risks adequately remain liable to regulatory action by the FCA

See Chapter 6 Section 7 of your Study Text

54. **C** Mitra should not have traded on the basis of this material, non-public information

See Chapter 9 Section 1 of your Study Text

55. **C** These are all examples of plagiarism, apart from using excerpts and quoting the source

See Chapter 9 Section 1 of your Study Text

56. **B** The worst scenario is for Rupert to go from paying no tax to paying the higher rate tax on the income from the gilts

See Chapter 12 Section 2 of your Study Text

57. **B** The Statement of Investment Principles is required to be prepared by the trustees

See Chapter 4 Section 8 of your Study Text

58. **C** The asset classes of cash, gilts and bonds are less likely than equities to provide the necessary capital growth that Bruce requires. Equities carry risk and so losses are possible, and volatility can be expected. We are asked which asset class produces the 'best chance'

See Chapter 10 Section 2 of your Study Text

59. **A** This is the definition of shortfall risk

See Chapter 10 Section 2.6.1 of your Study Text

60. **C** If life companies have sold annuities, they are subject to long-term regular cash outflows. Long term bonds provide long term regular inflows to match this

See Chapter 10 Section 3.3 of your Study Text

61. **D** Referral fees can lead to a conflict of interest but the requirement for disclosure should reduce this, as clients can then make up their own minds on the situation

See Chapter 9 Section 1 of your Study Text

62. **B** The best way of establishing affordability is to prepare a cashflow analysis, which can be in the form of an analysis of monthly household income and outgoings. This will establish whether the client's goals are realistic

See Chapter 10 Section 2.4 of your Study Text

63. **3.0** 3% is a material interest and would require a listed company to make an announcement to the market

See Chapter 2 Section 5.2 of your Study Text

64. **122000** The unused portion of the husband's tax-free band (here £312,000 − £499,200/2 = £62,400, which equates to 20%) is transferred to the wife. On her death the estate benefits from her tax-free band and the unused portion of his tax-free band at rates prevailing on the second death. Inheritance tax payable is (£695,000 − £325,000 × 120%) × 40% = £122,000

See Chapter 11 Section 4 of your Study Text

65. **B** The test for professional clients when carrying out non-MiFID business requires two of the following:

€12,500,000 balance sheet total

€25,000,000 net turnover

250 average number of employees in the year

So, the company would not be treated as a *per se* professional client and, as such, would be treated as a retail client

See Chapter 7 Section 1.6.4 of your Study Text

66. **A** While it is likely that the client satisfies the qualitative test, we are unable to show that he satisfy two of the criteria for the quantitative test, which are:

- The client has carried out at least ten 'significant' transactions per quarter on the relevant market, over the last four quarters

- The client's portfolio, including cash deposits, exceeds €500,000

- The client has knowledge of the transactions envisaged from at least one year's professional work in the financial sector

B&B must therefore treat Patrick as a retail client

See Chapter 7 Section 1.6.4 of your Study Text

67. **D** A record of the client agreement should be kept for five years, or for the duration of the relationship with the client, if longer. But, for pensions transfers, opt-outs, or FSAVCs, the record should be kept indefinitely

See Chapter 7 Section 1.9 of your Study Text

68. **C** COBS rules state that communications be clear, fair and not misleading

See Chapter 7 Section 2.4 of your Study Text

69. **D** Durable medium means that communication must be in paper or via any other instrument such as an email or fax which enables the recipient to store the information unchanged for later reproduction, such as by printing

See Chapter 7 Section 1.4 of your Study Text

70. **A** The IFA firm will normally be a client of the broker

See Chapter 7 Section 1.7 of your Study Text

71. **A** Gilts settle the same day or the next day, and so the best answer is T+1

See Chapter 2 Section 7.1 of your Study Text

72. **A** This depends on the type of pension fund since those with a young client base will tend to invest more heavily in equities while those with a more mature client base will typically make more use of bonds. However, UK pension funds invest heavily in bonds when considered overall

See Chapter 10 Section 3.2 of your Study Text

73. **D** Initially, a client should address the complaint with the firm. It might be that the client later takes the complaint to the Ombudsman but this is only if they do not achieve resolution with the firm

See Chapter 6 Section 8 of your Study Text

74. **D** The trustee is responsible for preparing the Statement of Funding Principles

See Chapter 4 Section 7.3 of your Study Text

75. **D** Providing safeguarding services is an ancillary service

See Chapter 1 Section 5.4 of your Study Text

76. **8.44** Net dividend = 12p per share

Net amount received = 7596p

Gross amount payable = 7596 × 100/90 = 8440p

Notional tax credit = 8440 − 7596 = 844p = £8.44

See Chapter 12 Section 1.4.1 of your Study Text

77. **C** Placement usually involves a deposit-taking institution.

See Chapter 6 Section 4.2 of your Study Text

78. **A** The mnemonic APRIL can help you to recall the list of exempt persons

A – Appointed representatives

P – Professions

R – Recognised institutions

I – Institutions (given special exemption)

L – Lloyds members

See Chapter 4 Section 4.5 of your Study Text

79. **B**   This option best describes the main aim behind the EU's drive for a single market in financial services

See Chapter 1 Section 4.9 of your Study Text

80. **C**   The Competition Commission might take up to 24 weeks to reach a decision

See Chapter 4 Section 2.4 of your Study Text

81. **C**   This is a general defence. Be sure to learn the general and special defences as separate lists

See Chapter 6 Section 5 of your Study Text

82. **B**   The Joint Money Laundering Steering Group Guidance Notes have been embraced by HMT and the FCA

See Chapter 6 Section 4.8 of your Study Text

83. **C**   The suitability rule applies to retail and professional clients

See Chapter 7 Section 3.1 of your Study Text

84. **C**   Firms must report twice a year. Nil returns are required

See Chapter 6 Section 8.8 of your Study Text

85. **C**   If a market maker is not prepared to deal, that in itself might lead to suspicions of something being announced. The market maker is required to act 'in good faith'. Since (in III) the client approaches the firm, the firm is allowed to conduct the trade, because again a refusal will arouse suspicions

See Chapter 7 Section 4 of your Study Text

PRACTICE EXAMINATION 2

(85 questions in 1 hour and 40 minutes)

1. Mrs Mandava is working in a investment bank and receives an unusual order for a deal of £50,000 from a relatively new client to transfer the monies recently placed in the account. What action should Mrs Mandava take?

    A   Inform the National Crime Agency (formerly the Serious Organised Crime Agency)

    B   Inform her line manager of her suspicions

    C   Inform her Money Laundering Reporting Officer

    D   Inform the Financial Conduct Authority

2. Four prospective clients may engage with your firm in business that is not MiFID or equivalent third country business.

    Which would be deemed to be a 'large undertaking'?

    A   Articall, a company with a €10m balance sheet total and €30m turnover

    B   Greenby Engineering, which has called-up share capital of £10m

    C   Mega-Mall Enterprises, with €12.5m balance sheet total and €20m turnover

    D   Landscape Print, which has €30m turnover and an average number of employees of 200 in the year

3. For which one of the following would a suitability report not be required?

    A   A pension transfer

    B   A decision to transfer to making income withdrawals from a short-term annuity

    C   Buy units in a regulated collective investment scheme

    D   If the firm acts as investment manager and recommends a regulated collective investment scheme

4. An individual has capital gains of £33,600 and income of £57,000. How much capital gains tax will be payable, to the nearest £? The annual exemption is £10,600.

    Important! You should enter only the answer in numbers (without spaces, letters or symbols) strictly using the following format: 0000

5. **A large company has decided to undertake a review of its responsibilities to its stakeholders. Which of the following might it reasonably conclude are among its stakeholders?**

      I   Employees

      II   Shareholders

      III   Suppliers

      IV   Customers

A II only

B I and II only

C I, II and IV only

D I, II, III and IV

6. **In the absence of knowledge of the recipient's suitability, cold (unsolicited) calls are allowed for**

      I   Authorised unit trusts

      II   Unauthorised unit trusts

      III   Derivatives

A I only

B II and III only

C I and III only

D I, II and III

7. **Your firm is conducting a review of its communications and has asked you to clarify the regulator's rules.**

When communicating with clients to satisfy rules stating that the communication be in durable form which of the following would be considered acceptable: email message, written letter, USB storage device, Compact Disc?

A None of the communication methods mentioned

B Email message, written letter or Compact Disc, but not USB storage device

C Email message or written letter, but not USB storage device or Compact Disc

D Email message, written letter, USB storage device and Compact Disc

8. **Mr Chang has decided to invest £50,000 into ordinary shares of a company for which he subsequently provides consultancy services, and he becomes privy to inside information. Which of the following courses of action is advisable for Mr Chang to take, in order to avoid breaching S118 FSMA 2000 on market abuse?**

A Mr Chang retains the shares

B Immediately, Mr Chang disposes of the shares

C Mr Chang declares to the market the information that he holds

D Mr Chang buys further shares in the company to close out his position

9.   **UCITS status allows for a fund**

   A   A passport across the EEA for collective investment schemes

   B   A passport across the EU for collective investment schemes

   C   To guarantee outperformance

   D   To guarantee lower charges and outperformance

10. **An individual dies leaving an estate on £319,000 to his children. In the previous year he had made gifts to them of £16,000. He made no other gifts in the previous seven years. How much inheritance tax is payable?**

   A   £1,800

   B   £1,600

   C   £720

   D   Nil

11. **Variation margin, as calculated by LCH.Clearnet for trades on NYSE Liffe, refers to**

   A   The maximum probable loss on a single day

   B   The likely loss for the week ahead

   C   The actual loss for the previous week

   D   The mark to market gain / loss on the position on the previous day

12. **Which of the following is not an offence under insider dealing legislation?**

   A   Dealing in shares when in possession of inside information

   B   Encouraging another person to deal when in possession of inside information

   C   Dealing as a market maker when in possession of inside information

   D   Disclosing inside information to another person

13. **Graham W. is an analyst who becomes aware of price-sensitive inside information that is not available to the general public. Which of the following courses of action by Graham would not amount to market abuse in this case?**

   A   Recommend to clients that they trade in the security concerned

   B   Take no further action

   C   Switch discretionary funds under the firm's management into this security

   D   Recommend to clients that they do not trade in the security concerned

14. **Which of the following is correct regarding the appointment of a proxy at a company general meeting?**

   A   The proxy is valid for the meeting but not for any adjournment

   B   A general proxy may vote as he thinks fit, considering anything that is discussed at the meeting

   C   A proxy is unable to vote on a show of hands

   D   A proxy does not have the right to speak

15. **A UK-listed mortgage lender operates through agents in a number of foreign countries. The lender has identified bribery risks associated with its reliance on agents and is considering**

what action it should take to ensure compliance with anti-bribery legislation. Which of the following is not an appropriate measure for the firm to adopt in pursuit of this objective?

A   Explain its intentions to strengthen anti-bribery procedures through written communications to all of its agents

B   Provide for its staff a confidential channel of communication through which to raise any concerns they may have about bribery

C   Include in its procedures manual a disclaimer of responsibility for any actions of its agents in which bribery is involved where they are based outside the UK

D   Communicate its anti-bribery message periodically through external channels such as trade publications and industry fairs

16.   You are working for a new employer. Your firm operates a suspicious transaction reporting system which identifies suspicious transactions for further investigation by a number of criteria, including the amount of the transaction. You have been assigned to work in the department that investigates these transactions.

Selina, your supervisor, has explained that external auditors often test samples of transactions in order to assess whether errors may be 'material' to the business of the firm. Selina routinely disregards most items on the report. She proposes that, given time pressures, you should adopt a similar approach to investigating the suspicious transactions: she tells you to pick one out of ten transactions randomly, for further investigation.

What should you do, taking into account ethical requirements?

A   Investigate all of the cases of suspicious transactions reported, while telling the Compliance Department of Selina's proposed procedure

B   Report Selina's actions to the regulatory authority

C   Follow Selina's approach, since most of the transactions are small relative to the size of the firm

D   Follow Selina's approach, since commercial realities must be balanced with regulatory compliance

17.   According to the UKLA Listing Rules, what is the minimum market capitalisation for a listed company on issue of equity?

A   At least £300,000

B   At least £500,000

C   At least £700,000

D   At least £1,000,000

18.   In the context of authorisation by the regulator, which of the following is an exempt person?

A   Recognised Investment Exchange

B   Employee share scheme

C   Dealing as principal

D   Overseas person

19. **Clive Woodley (CW) is a professional client who requests to opt down to be afforded greater protection in its dealings with your firm.**

    Which one of the following applies?

    A   CW can be treated as a retail customer without notification

    B   CW can be categorised as a retail customer but must be notified by the firm

    C   CW cannot opt down

    D   The firm must pay attention to the experience, expertise and knowledge of CW before deciding if the client can opt down

20. **Carl, a financial adviser, has approached Andy to discuss pensions following a referral from Carl's customer, Peter. Andy asks who suggested that he might be interested in pensions.**

    What should Carl do?

    A   Decline to answer Andy's question

    B   Give Peter's name, having obtained his permission at the outset to do so

    C   Give Peter's name and explain briefly the nature of Peter's business with the company

    D   State that he must first obtain his client's permission to reveal his name

21. **Your firm is reviewing the financial promotions that it issues. Which of the following financial promotions would not fall under the territorial scope of the FCA's Financial Promotions regulations?**

    A   A financial promotion made to an investor based in the UK

    B   An unwritten cold call made to an investor based outside of the UK

    C   Approving a financial promotion of an overseas person communicated at investors in the UK

    D   A solicited unwritten financial promotion made to an overseas person

22. **The application of Jarrow Smith Advisers for a change in permission is refused by the FCA. To whom can the firm appeal?**

    A   TCCUT

    B   RDC

    C   FCA

    D   HMT

23. **Which one of the following is not classified as a regulated activity?**

    A   Accepting deposits

    B   Lloyd's market-related activities

    C   Sending dematerialised instructions

    D   Dealing as a principal (where not holding oneself out to the market)

24. **What is the most important consequence for regulated firms of the FCA's adoption of a 'principles-based' approach to regulation?**

A Firms should have fewer detailed FCA rules to follow but must follow higher-level principles

B Firms must formulate a set of principles and must disclose these principles to private customers before they do business

C Firms can expect more regular compliance checks from the FCA, whether or not their activities are regarded as risky

D Firms will decide which detailed rules to follow based on whether the rules are in accord with the firm's principles

25. **Which of the following is not a *per se* eligible counterparty?**

A Insurance company

B Pension fund

C Central Bank

D Treasury department of a large oil company

26. **The Office of Fair Trading may refer a merger to the Competition Commission if the merger adds to or creates a market share of**

A 10% or more

B 20% or more

C 25% or more

D 30% or more

27. **Which of the following would be general defences to the charge of insider dealing under Criminal Justice Act 1993?**

   I   Not expecting to make a profit

   II   Dealing only in treasury bonds

   III Believed the information was published

A I and III only

B II only

C II and III only

D I, II and III

28. **What best describes the purpose of the client categorisation rules?**

A To ensure that those who take most risk receive the most protection

B To ensure that clients receive the correct protection given their level of knowledge and understanding

C To enable firms to decide which rules are applicable

D To assist with decisions relating to client money

29. **How long must a firm keep its records on the scope and ranges of products on which it advises, in relation to its MiFID business?**

A One year

B Three years

C Five years

D Six years

30. **When implementing the 'Best execution criteria' the firm must take into account all of the following characteristics, except**

A The client order

B How long the client has been a client of the firm

C The execution venues

D The financial instruments

31. **For business that is not MiFID or equivalent third country business, confirmations need not be supplied if the designated investment is a**

A SIPP

B Derivative

C Life policy

D Share of a single company

32. **Which of the following types of bond pays a semi-annual coupon?**

A French government bonds

B German government bonds

C Japanese government bonds

D Eurobonds

33. **Which of the following can the shareholders normally do at an AGM?**

I Approve the accounts

II Remove the directors

III Change the amount of the dividend

A I only

B I and II only

C I and III only

D I, II and III

34. **Which one of the following are a permitted power for a small trust under the Trustee Act 2000?**

I Purchase overseas land

II Purchase ordinary shares

III Purchase corporate bonds

A I and II only

B I only

C II and III only

D I, II, and III

35. An investor, who is a higher rate taxpayer, buys two investments, generating a chargeable gain of £11,500. Assuming a CGT annual exemption of £10,600, calculate the capital gains tax payable in £.

    Important! You should enter only the answer in numbers (without spaces, letters or symbols) strictly using the following format: 000

    ```
    [                              ]
    ```

36. Victoria and Kevin are advisers who have each spent time during the last week making some unsolicited calls ('cold calls') to prospective clients. Both advisers have been in their roles for one year, and are working for the same firm, with the same supervisor. The supervisor has reviewed their cold calling practices and found that Victoria's calls contravened the regulators' rules on call calling, while Kevin's appeared to be compliant.

    Which of the following alternative scenarios could explains the supervisor's review findings?

    A   Victoria's calls related to self-invested personal pensions. Kevin's calls related to stakeholder pension plans

    B   Victoria and Kevin were both calling prospective clients about the same product type. Kevin made his calls between 10am and 4pm on weekdays. Victoria's calls were at various times, including Saturday and Sunday evenings between 9pm and 10pm

    C   Victoria's calls related to life policies. Kevin's calls related to investment trust savings schemes

    D   Victoria's and Kevin's were all to prospective clients about a new range of unit trusts that their firm has added to the list of products on which it gives advice. Victoria's calls related to making an investment within child trust funds. Kevin's calls related to making an investment outside tax wrappers

37. Which of the following activities are not covered under the Financial Services and Markets Act?

    A   Acting as a broker
    B   Accepting deposits
    C   Giving investment advice
    D   Acting as an unremunerated trustee

38. Which of the following is true of the Financial Ombudsman Service?

    I   Firms are required to cooperate with the Financial Ombudsman Service
    II   There is no limit on the amount which the FOS can require a firm pays to a complainant
    III   If the FOS makes a decision which the complainant wishes to enforce then it is binding on the firm

    A   I, II and III
    B   I only
    C   III only
    D   I and III only

39. Which of the following is not among the entities eligible to bring a 'super complaint' or mass detriment reference to the FCA?

    A   A group of at least 100 consumers
    B   A consumer body designated to do so by HM Treasury
    C   The Financial Ombudsman Service
    D   An authorised firm

40. A direct offer financial promotion might be best described as an offer to

    A   Enter into an agreement with a high net worth individual without receiving further information
    B   Discuss an agreement with a new potential customer without receiving further information
    C   Investors to purchase investments directly 'off-the-page' without receiving further information
    D   Extend an agreement with an existing customer without receiving further information

41. Which of the following provides a route to authorisation under the Financial Services and Markets Act?

    I   Permission from the FCA
    II   Membership of a designated professional body
    III   Authorisation to carry out investment business in a member state of the EU (other than the UK)
    IV   Authorisations to carry out investment business in the United States

    A   I and II only
    B   I and III only
    C   I, II and III only
    D   I, II, III and IV

42. Giuliana is a financial adviser with the authorised firm Compass 360 Advisers. One of Giuliana's clients wishes to discuss building a portfolio of direct stock market investments. Giuliana's experience is almost entirely within the area of insurance-based products and she does not feel confident about the areas of investment that the client wishes to discuss, although she is authorised to do so. What should Giuliana do?

    A   Offer advice at a 'basic' level and ask the client to sign that they have received an appropriate disclaimer
    B   Propose a meeting jointly with the client and another adviser within the firm who has more relevant experience
    C   State clearly that she is unable to act and apologise to the client for any inconvenience
    D   Persuade the client to consider the product types of which she has more experience

43. What is the name of the German settlement system?

    A   Clearstream
    B   CEDEL
    C   CREST
    D   EUREX

44. **When may a firm make cold (unsolicited) calls?**

A   Between 08:30 and 20:30 Monday to Friday

B   When the recipient has an established client relationship with the firm such that the recipient envisages receiving such calls

C   Between 09:00 and 20:00 Monday to Saturday

D   When the recipient has requested the call

---

45. **Which of the following statements about periodic statements are correct?**

I   They must include the name/designation of a retail client's account

II   They must include the name of the firm

III   For a retail client, they are required semi-annually for a securities portfolio

IV   For a retail client involved in a leveraged portfolio, they should be provided once every three months

A   I and III only

B   II and IV only

C   III only

D   I, II and III only

---

46. **Which of the following is an exempt person under the Financial Services and Markets Act?**

A   A person authorised in another EU state

B   The London Stock Exchange

C   The Law Society

D   The New York Stock Exchange

---

47. **As a member of a professional body in the financial services industry, you have agreed to its Code of Ethics. As an approved person, you are subject to the regulatory requirements.**

What is the best description of how you will act in an ethical manner?

A   You will make sure that you have passed all appropriate examinations and that your approved person status is maintained

B   You will act in accordance with the wishes of your client at all times, above all else

C   You will act in accordance with your commitment to the highest standards of personal ethics and integrity in carrying out professional work

D   You will act in accordance with all of the regulator's rules on business conduct

---

48. **An individual dies leaving an estate of £340,000 that is left to his civil partner. How much inheritance tax is payable?**

A   £136,000

B   £11,200

C   £16,000

D   Nil

49. Harry Yeung dies leaving half of his £436,800 estate to his children and the rest to his wife, when the inheritance tax nil rate band is £312,000. Three years later, Harry's wife dies, leaving a total estate of £478,000 to their children when the nil rate band is £340,000. How much inheritance tax will be payable on the wife's death?

    A £14,400

    B £55,200

    C £142,560

    D £105,120

50. Which of the following is most appropriately described as a returns-maximising fund?

    A Defined benefit pension fund

    B Life assurance fund

    C Open ended investment company

    D General insurance fund

51. Which of the following are nominal liabilities?

    I Mortgage principal

    II Index-linked pension

    III Credit card balance

    A I and II only

    B I and III only

    C II and III only

    D I, II and III

52. What effect will a shorter timescale have on the risk attitude of a fund?

    A No change

    B Increase risk tolerance

    C Reduce risk tolerance

    D Reduce risk implications

53. A house is bought for £287,000. What will be the stamp duty land tax payable by the buyer?

    A Nil

    B £8,610

    C £1,111

    D £5,740

54. Who is responsible for regulating recognised clearing houses?

    A The Bank of England

    B HM Treasury

    C The Financial Conduct Authority

    D The Prudential Regulation Authority

55.   If the outcome of a Financial Services Ombudsman investigation is accepted by the complainant, then it is

A   At the discretion of the firm to comply

B   Implemented by HMT

C   Binding on the firm

D   Binding on the customer

56.   Which of the following dealings is not covered by the insider dealing legislation?

A   Trading in a Eurobond with the aim of price stabilisation

B   Trading in shares on a foreign stock exchange where those shares are listed on the LSE

C   Trading in advertised securities off a recognised exchange

D   Trading in shares in a recognised exchange other than the LSE

57.   Which of the following would be an offence under the provisions of the insider dealing legislation?

A   A predator company buying shares in the target company prior to announcement of the bid

B   An individual using inside information to their advantage but not from a known source

C   A person using inside information but not to gain a profit or avoid a loss

D   An institutional investor buying shares without having announced their intention to do so

The following information relates to questions 58 to 63

Samson Industries is a manufacturer of sporting equipment who currently control 14% of the market. They hope to take over Delilah Sporting Goods which has a market value of £60 million; its shares are currently trading at £2.60. Samson Industries intends to offer £3.00 per share to Delilah shareholders. Samson aims to purchase all shares in the Delilah.

58.   Which is the maximum market share Delilah could have control of that would be likely to avoid the OFT instigating an investigation?

A   10%

B   5%

C   15%

D   25%

59.   If the OFT did decide that an investigation were needed, this is most likely to be carried out by

A   The OFT

B   The Competition Commission

C   The FCA

D   The Takeover Panel

60. **What is the Takeover Panel levy payable by the seller of £310,000 of shares through the LSE? Give your answer in pounds and pence.**

Important! You should enter only the answer in numbers (without spaces, letters or symbols) strictly using the following format: 00.00

```
```

61. **Under the terms of the Takeover Code, what is the least time that Samson must leave the offer on the table for Delilah shareholders before they can remove their bid?**

A 14 days

B 21 days

C 28 days

D 60 days

62. **The shareholders of Delilah prove unenthusiastic about the offer and the number of shareholders accepting the bid falls short of that required by Samson. After 60 days, Samson withdraws its bid. How long will it be before Samson is able to make a further bid?**

A 90 days

B 6 months

C 1 year

D 10 years

63. **What is the least percentage (%) of shares that Samson will need to purchase to guarantee that they can buy all of the Delilah shares?**

Important! You should enter only the answer in numbers (without spaces, letters or symbols) strictly using the following format: 00

```
```

64. **The maximum sentence for an individual failing to report suspicions of money laundering is**

A 14 years' imprisonment

B 7 years' imprisonment

C 5 years' imprisonment

D 2 years' imprisonment

65. **On summary conviction under the Insider Dealing Act, the maximum penalty is**

A One year's imprisonment

B Seven years' imprisonment and a fine of up to the statutory maximum

C Seven years' imprisonment

D Six months' imprisonment and a fine of up to the statutory maximum

66. **For a new retail client in respect of designated investment business, when must a firm provide the retail client with the terms of the agreement they are obliged to provide?**

    A Within five business days of starting business

    B Normally before the client is bound by any agreement

    C It is not necessary to provide the terms of agreement

    D Immediately after the client is bound by the agreement, no matter how the agreement was concluded

67. **When must an authorised firm assess appropriateness?**

    A When executing a warrants transaction for a retail client as a result of a direct offer financial promotion

    B For a life insurance investment when the client has declined advice

    C For an authorised collective investment scheme

    D For all transactions with retail clients

68. **If an investor earning £80,000 receives a net UK dividend of £600, what additional tax is payable?**

    A £120

    B £150

    C £135

    D £67

69. **You have taken over a list of 30 clients from an adviser who has recently left your firm. In one case, it is clear to you that investments have been switched in order to generate additional commissions. In another case, investments have been included in a client's portfolio that are unsuitable in the light of the client's risk profile, in order to generate higher commissions. Which of the following actions or sets of actions is most appropriate in these circumstances?**

    A Review approximately ten further clients' files and, if they all appear satisfactory, treat the two dubious cases as isolated incidents and take no further action

    B Raise the issue with a supervisor or senior manager so that a full review of this adviser's client list can be implemented, and compensate the clients for losses arising from the unsuitable investments

    C Raise the issue with a supervisor or senior manager so that a full review of this adviser's client list can be implemented; contact the providers of the mis-sold products and demand that they compensate the clients

    D Contact the providers of the mis-sold products and demand that they compensate the clients; review approximately ten further clients' files and, if they all appear satisfactory, treat the two dubious cases as isolated incidents

70. **Which organisation will deal with a company's application to join the UK Official List?**

    A Bank of England

    B Department of Business, Innovation and Skills

    C United Kingdom Listing Authority

    D London Stock Exchange

71. **Which of the following would not be deemed to be a criminal activity?**

    A Avoiding tax

    B Tax evasion

    C Forgery

    D Drug trafficking

72. **Which of the following would make an EU directive effective in the UK?**

    I   The UK Parliament passing primary legislation

    II   The UK Parliament adapting existing legislation

    III   The EU issuing regulations altering UK laws

    IV   An individual successfully taking the matter to the European Court

    A I, II and III only

    B I, II and IV only

    C I, II, III and IV

    D I and II only

73. **Under the CFA Code and Principles, which of the following is the most correct course of action if an order for multiple clients is not filled?**

    A Fill the order of the biggest client first

    B Fill the order of the smallest client first

    C Fill the order of the clients how have recently suffered losses first

    D Fill the orders on a pro-rata basis

74. **Which of the following are 'packaged products'?**

    I   Life policy

    II   Units in a regulated CIS

    III   An interest in an investment trust savings scheme

    A I and III only

    B II and III only

    C II only

    D I, II and III

75. The Compliance Officer at QWR Investors is drafting a procedures manual for the firm's investment advisers. Among other topics, the manual will set out to enable advisers to understand the main FCA principles, rules and requirements relating to the provision of investment advice and product disclosure, including in relation to the assessment of client suitability requirements.

    When preparing suitability reports to comply with the regulator's rules, which of the following is not correct?

    A A suitability report will need to be prepared if basic scripted advice is given on a stakeholder product

    B If a personal pension plan is recommended, an explanation should be included of why it is at least as suitable as a stakeholder pension

    C Suitability should result from keeping to the 'know your customer' rule

    D A suitability report is required when the firm makes a recommendation and the client enters into a pension transfer

76. **A basic written agreement concerning designated investment business is always required for**

    A An eligible counterparty

    B An eligible client

    C A professional client

    D A retail client

77. **Which of the following types of investment business require authorisation?**

        I   Bonds

        II   Shares

        III   Options on shares

    A I and II only

    B I only

    C III only

    D I, II and III

78. **Which of the following are part of the criteria that the FCA would consider when looking to test the fitness and propriety of an approved person?**

        I   Honesty, integrity and reputation

        II   Competence and capability

        III   Financial soundness

    A I only

    B I and II only

    C II and III only

    D I, II and III

79. Gail Faulkner is preparing a research report on a small biotech company for public distribution. Her supervisor sees a rough draft with favourable earnings projections. Faulkner later obtains revised data and lowers the favourable projections. Just before the report is published, Faulkner sees that her supervisor has substituted her earlier, more favourable projections in place of the less favourable projections. According to CFA Institute Code and Standards Faulkner should

A Immediately report the incident to the regulatory authorities

B Require either inclusion of the unfavourable earnings projections or removal of her name from the report

C Request that the report include a disclaimer with respect to the earnings projections

D Allow the report to be distributed without revision, but prepare and release a second report that includes the lower earnings projection

80. Which of the following are not exempt under the Financial Promotions Order?

A Journalists writing share advice columns

B Financial promotions communicated only to members of the Designated Professional Bodies

C Financial promotions communicated only to investment professionals

D A one-off promotion to existing customers

81. Which two of the following are 'core' investment services and activities under MiFID?

    I   Receipt and transmission of orders

    II   Advising on mergers and acquisitions

    III Discretionary management of investment portfolios

    IV   Safeguarding and administration of financial instruments

A I and II

B III and IV

C I and III

D II and IV

82. When treating a retail client as an elective professional client for a transaction, an investment manager should

    I   Assess the client has adequate expertise, experience and knowledge

    II   Assess the client is capable of making his own investment decisions

    III Assess the client understands the risks involved

A I only

B II and III only

C I and III only

D I, II and III

83. **Which of the following are among the basic aims of insolvency law?**

    I   Balancing the interests of competing groups

    II   Protect the shareholders of the company

    III Encourage 'rescue' operations

A II only

B I and III only

C I and III only

D I, II and III

84. **Malcolm Janner is a consultant for ABB Securities. In the course of his work he becomes aware of inside information. Which of the following would not be a breach of the market abuse regime?**

A He discloses the inside information to the market

B Having been asked to do so, he discloses the inside information to the relevant regulator

C He uses the information to transact in ABC plc securities

D He encourages a friend to transact in ABC securities based on the inside information

85. **With regard to investigations by the FCA, the regulator may**

    I   Require the authorised firms and its employees to provide all documents to the investigation team that they deem relevant

    II   Require the authorised firms and its employees to attend a questioning by an investigator and require the person to answer questions

    III Appoint accountants, actuaries and other professionals to do a one-off investigation into the firm's activities

    IV Extend its investigation beyond the regulated activities of the firm

A I and IV only

B I, II, III and IV

C III only

D I, II and III only

Answers

1. **C** If a person suspects a person of money laundering they should inform the police or an appropriate officer. This person is usually the MLRO

    See Chapter 6 Section 4.7.2 of your Study Text

2. **B** In this question the business is not MiFID business, so we are looking for two out of the three limits: €12,500,000 balance sheet total, €25,000,000 net turnover, and 250 average number of employees in the year. Options A, C and D satisfy two of these limits. Alternatively, called up share capital of at least £5,000,000 qualifies an undertaking as 'large'

    See Chapter 7 Section 1.6 of your Study Text

3. **D** A suitability report would not be required where a firm is acting as investment manager and recommends a regulated collective investment scheme. Be aware of when a suitability report is, and is not, required

    See Chapter 7 Section 3.2.1 of your Study Text

4. **6440** (£33,600 – £10,600) = £23,000. £23,000 × 28% = £6,440

    See Chapter 11 Section 3 of your Study Text

5. **D** Large companies are increasingly being held to account for their interactions with all groups who their activities touch

    See Chapter 9 Section 2.13 of your Study Text

6. **A** Firms are restricted in what they can sell through cold calls. They are permitted for generally marketed packaged products not based on a high volatility fund

    See Chapter 7 Section 2.13 of your Study Text

7. **D** 'Durable medium' means that communication must be in paper or via any other instrument such as an email or fax which enables the recipient to store the information unchanged for later reproduction

    See Chapter 7 Section 1.4 of your Study Text

8. **A** Since Mr Chang was not an insider when the investment was made, there has been no breach of S118. On becoming an insider, there is no need to dispose of the shares, nor is there is a need to declare information to the market. The option to close out the position (D) is a distractor that does not make sense

    See Chapter 6 Section 6.1 of your Study Text

9. **A** UCITS III allows funds to be passported across the EEA

    See Chapter 1 Section 6.1 of your Study Text

10.　**B**　Inheritance tax is payable on the death estate plus the lifetime transfers within seven years of death

	£
Taxable transfer	
Life time transfer in last seven years	
– Last year	16,000
Annual gift exemption	
– Last year	(3,000)
– Year before carried forward	(3,000)
(can carry forward on year)	
	10,000
Death estate	319,000
Taxable transfer	329,000

Inheritance tax payable	£
£325,000 at 0%	0
£4,000 at 40%	1,600
Total	1,600

See Chapter 11 Section 4 of your Study Text

11.　**D**　Variation margin represents the daily profits or losses incurred on an investor's positions. The revaluing of these positions is often referred to as marking-to-market

See Chapter 2 Section 3.2 of your Study Text

12.　**C**　Market makers carry out their normal business is a special defence

See Chapter 6 Section 5.5.1 of your Study Text

13.　**B**　There are seven offences that relate to market abuse. Taking no further action is an appropriate way for an analyst to deal with such a situation and is not an offence of market abuse

See Chapter 6 Section 6.1 of your Study Text

14.　**B**　A proxy is valid for the meeting and any adjournment. The ability to vote either way is known as a general proxy. Following CA 2006 changes, proxies may exercise all the powers the member would have if they were present in person, including the right to speak, and to vote on a show of hands or on a poll

See Chapter 2 Section 5.8.5 of your Study Text

15.　**C**　A, B and D may all serve to promote proportionate anti-bribery procedures, in line with the Bribery Act 2010. A disclaimer of responsibility (C) is likely to be ineffective and does not form part of 'adequate procedures' as required by the anti-bribery legislation

See Chapter 6 Section 7 of your Study Text

16.　**A**　The suspicious transactions report identifies transactions for further investigation, and so you should investigate each one. Financial crime compliance requirements impose requirements that firms will investigate suspicious transactions, and materiality to the business is not relevant

See Chapter 9 Section 2 of your Study Text

17.　**C**　Shares at least £700,000; debt at least £200,000

See Chapter 2 Section 4.2 of your Study Text

18. **A** RIEs are exempt from the need to be authorised. All the others are types of excluded activities. Make sure you are clear as to who are 'exempt persons' and what are the 'excluded activities'

See Chapter 4 Section 2.5 of your Study Text

19. **B** If a professional client requests to opt down, then the firm must allow this

See Chapter 7 Section 1.6.1 of your Study Text

20. **B** The name of the person making the referral should be given to the client

See Chapter 7 Section 1 of your Study Text

21. **D** As the overseas person has solicited the unwritten communication, the FCA rules do not apply. The rules only apply outside the UK in relation to financial promotions that are cold calls

See Chapter 7 Section 2 of your Study Text

22. **A** The firm has a right to appeal to the Tribunal (TCCUT)

See Chapter 5 Section 3.4 of your Study Text

23. **D** The requirement to seek authorisation does not apply to personal dealings of unauthorised persons for their own account, hence an excluded activity

See Chapter 4 Section 4.6 of your Study Text

24. **A** The 'principles-based' approach goes hand-in-hand with the 'risk-based' approach. There should be fewer detailed rules and more emphasis on higher-level principles

See Chapter 9 Section 2.11.2 of your Study Text

25. **D** The Treasury department of a large oil company would be treated as a professional client. It could, if it so requests, be treated as an elective eligible counterparty but only with respect of eligible counterparty business. The others are individual in the list of per se eligible counterparties

See Chapter 7 Section 1.6.5 of your Study Text

26. **C** Or the target company turnover is greater than, or equal to, £70m, as this is 'a substantial lessening of competition'

See Chapter 4 Section 2.4 of your Study Text

27. **A** The CJA 1993 provides three statutory general defences for insider dealing. Dealing in treasury bonds is not one of them

See Chapter 6 Section 5.4 of your Study Text

28. **B** This is the main purpose. Clearly C is a consequence of categorising clients but it is not the main purpose of the rule

See Chapter 7 Section 1.6 of your Study Text

29. **C** The record keeping requirement in relation to MiFID business is five years

See Chapter 6 Section 3.1 of your Study Text

30. **B** The length of time a client has been a client of the firm is not relevant

See Chapter 7 Section 7.2 of your Study Text

31. **C** All of the others require a confirmation note to be sent

See Chapter 6 Section 3.2 of your Study Text

32. **C** The JGB pays semi-annual coupon, as does the US 'T'-Bond, the UK gilt and the Italian BTP. French OATs, German bunds and Eurobonds all pay annual coupon

See Chapter 2 Section 7.1 of your Study Text

33. **B** At the Annual General Meeting (AGM), the shareholders can approve or reject the proposed dividend, approve the accounts, reappoint directors and reappoint auditors. However, they cannot change the dividend that has been proposed by the directors

See Chapter 2 Section 5.7 of your Study Text

34. **C** The only asset class not allowed is overseas land

See Chapter 4 Section 6.2 of your Study Text

35. **252** Chargeable gain   £11,500

Less annual exemption   (10,600)

Gain subject to CGT   £900

The higher rate for CGT is 28%, making a CGT liability of £252

See Chapter 11 Section 3 of your Study Text

36. **B** Cold calls are permitted for both SIPPs (a type of personal pension plan) and stakeholder pension plans: these are packaged products. Although the regulator does not lay down specific permitted times of day for cold calls, it is stipulated that calls should be made at 'an appropriate time of day'. Calls between 9pm and 10pm at weekends could be considered inappropriate. Cold calls are permitted for both life policies and investment trust savings plans: these are packaged products

See Chapter 7 Section 2.13 of your Study Text

37. **D** Trustees where they are not deemed to be experts, holding themselves out to the general public, and are not separately remunerated are excluded from the requirement to seek authorisation

See Chapter 4 Section 4.6 of your Study Text

38. **D** FCA-authorised firms are required to participate in the Financial Ombudsman Scheme and to cooperate with the Ombudsman. The firm is bound by the Ombudsman's decision if the client enforces it

See Chapter 6 Section 9 of your Study Text

39. **A** Designated consumer bodies may bring super-complaints, while the FOS and regulated firms may bring mass detriment references

See Chapter 6 Section 8.9 of your Study Text

40.   **C**   A direct offer financial promotion must contain appropriate disclosures and for non-MiFID business additional information so that the client is reasonably able to understand the risks and make investment decisions on an informed basis

See Chapter 7 Section 2.12 of your Study Text

41.   **B**   Membership of a designated professional body exempts an entity from the requirement to seek authorisation if the regulated activities it conducts are incidental to its main business

See Chapter 4 Section 4.4 of your Study Text

42.   **B**   The adviser should aim to ensure that the client is still assisted by the firm

See Chapter 9 Section 2 of your Study Text

43.   **A**   The German settlement system is Clearstream

See Chapter 2 Section 7.6.1 of your Study Text

44.   **B**   A call cannot be described as a 'cold call' if the recipient requested the call. There are no set time limits in COBS for when cold calls can be made

See Chapter 7 Section 2.13 of your Study Text

45.   **D**   In the case of a leveraged portfolio, it should be sent out once a month

See Chapter 6 Section 3.6 of your Study Text

46.   **B**   The LSE is one of the Recognised Investment Exchanges, and therefore exempt from the requirement to seek authorisation

See Chapter 4 Section 4.5 of your Study Text

47.   **C**   Exam passes and approved person status do not make you act ethically (Option A). Sometimes other legal requirements, such as to report suspicions of money laundering or other financial crime, must override your duty to a client, including the duty to act with confidentiality (Option B). Acting ethically involves more than compliance with rules (Option D)

See Chapter 9 Section 1 of your Study Text

48.   **D**   Inheritance tax is not payable when the estate passes to a spouse or civil partner

See Chapter 11 Section 4.5.1 of your Study Text

49.   **A**   The unused portion of the husband's tax-free band (here £312,000 − (£436,800/2)) = £93,600, which equates to 30% of the nil rate band) is transferred to the wife. On the wife's death, the estate benefits from her tax-free band and the unused portion of his tax-free band at rates prevailing on the second death. Inheritance tax payable is (£478, 000 − (£340,000 × 130%)) × 40% = £14,400

See Chapter 11 Section 4 of your Study Text

50.   **C**   The others primarily match liabilities

See Chapter 10 Section 2.2 of your Study Text

51.   **B**   An index-linked pension is a real liability as it will rise as inflation rises and is not fixed in cash (nominal) terms

See Chapter 10 Section 2.3 of your Study Text

52.   **C**   Shorter timescales lead to a reduced risk tolerance and increases the potential impacts of any risks

See Chapter 10 Section 2.6.4 of your Study Text

53.   **B**   Stamp duty land tax will be payable at 3% on the full purchase proceeds

See Chapter 11 Section 6.1.2 of your Study Text

54.   **A**   Following the changes introduced in the Financial Services Act 2012, the Bank of England has responsibility for regulating settlement systems and recognised clearing houses (RCHs)

See Chapter 2 Section 3.4 of your Study Text

55.   **C**   The firm must comply

See Chapter 3 Section 5.4 of your Study Text

56.   **A**   Stabilisation is a specific exemption and will not constitute insider dealing

See Chapter 6 Section 5.5.3 of your Study Text

57.   **B**   This is the best answer as the individual does not need to know the exact source, just that it was an inside source

See Chapter 6 Section 5 of your Study Text

58.   **A**   The OFT would be likely to investigate if the combined enterprise controlled at least 25%. If Samson controls 14%, this suggests that an investigation should be avoided if Delilah controls 10%

See Chapter 4 Section 2.2.2 of your Study Text

59.   **B**   The Competition Commission would investigate following an OFT report

See Chapter 4 Section 2.3 of your Study Text

60.   **01.00**   The levy is £1 for both buyers and sellers of £1 on transactions over £10,000

See Chapter 4 Section 2.1 of your Study Text

61.   **B**   The first day that a bid may close is Day 21. If it then goes 'unconditional' then the offer must remain on the table for further 14 days

See Chapter 4 Section 3.4 of your Study Text

62.   **C**   Once a bid has lapsed, the bidding company may not launch a further bid for at least one year

See Chapter 4 Section 3.4 of your Study Text

63.   **90**   At 90% a company may invoke a compulsory purchase order, which forces any minority shareholders to sell their share

See Chapter 4 Section 3.4 of your Study Text

64.   **C**   Five years, assuming a Crown Court sentence

See Chapter 6 Section 4.6.2 of your Study Text

65.   **D**   Summary proceedings take place in a Magistrates' Court

See Chapter 6 Section 5.7 of your Study Text

66. **B** An agreement must be provided immediately only if the agreement was concluded using a means of distance communication, so the best answer is that it should be provided before the client is bound by any agreement

   See Chapter 7 Section 1.9 of your Study Text

67. **A** Appropriateness rules will apply to executing a deal in derivatives in response to a direct offer promotion

   See Chapter 7 Section 3.3 of your Study Text

68. **B** **Step 1:** Calculate the gross dividend

   £600 × 100/90 = £666.67

   Step 2: Calculate amount the high rate taxpayer should pay in full on this account

   £666.67 × 32.5% = £216.67

   Step 3: Deduct 10% tax already deducted at source

   £216.67 – £66.67 = **£150**

   Note that the 32.5% rate was applied as this is a higher rate taxpayer, but he is not above the additional rate income level where dividends are taxed at 42.5%

   See Chapter 11 Section 1.3.5 of your Study Text

69. **B** Even if these are the only two cases, the clients have lost money and further action should be taken. It appears unlikely that the product provider could be held liable

   See Chapter 9 Section 2 of your Study Text

70. **C** The UK Listing Authority (UKLA) is responsible for allowing firms onto the official list, and hence becoming 'listed' companies. The UKLA is a part of the FCA

   See Chapter 2 Section 4.1 of your Study Text

71. **A** Minimising your tax liability through 'tax avoidance' is not a criminal activity. However, HMRC may challenge tax avoidance schemes that go beyond efficient tax planning and may seek to defeat it through the Courts

   See Chapter 11 Section 5.4 of your Study Text

72. **C** A European directive requires that a government either amends existing legislation or imposes new legislation in their own state to cover the regulations laid out in the directive. EU Regulations can take direct effect (ie without implementing measures by the member state)

   See Chapter 1 Section 4.2.3 of your Study Text

73. **D** The CFA Code and Standards require that trade allocation is carried out on a fair basis. The *pro rata* allocation is the only fair allocation method described

   See Chapter 9 Section 1 of your Study Text

74. **D** The definition of packaged products includes personal and stakeholder pensions and all of those listed

   See Chapter 7 Section 5.1 of your Study Text

75. **A** A suitability report is not required in the case of the 'basic' level of advice on stakeholder products

See Chapter 7 Section 3.2 of your Study Text

76. **D** It is only required for a retail client

See Chapter 7 Section 1.9 of your Study Text

77. **D** All three are types of specified investments and are all types of investment business. (Note that 'investment business' is not a defined term in FCA regulations)

See Chapter 4 Section 4.11 of your Study Text

78. **D** All of these would be considered

See Chapter 6 Section 1.1 and 1.2 of your Study Text

79. **B** Standard I.D – Misconduct states that members shall not engage in any professional conduct involving dishonesty, fraud, deceit, or misrepresentation or commit any act that reflects adversely on their honesty, trustworthiness or professional competence. Faulkner should insist that the most recent, less favourable projections be included in the report

See Chapter 9 Section 1.3 of your Study Text

80. **B** Journalists are not carrying out the activity 'in the course of investment business'. Members of DPBs are not necessarily investment professionals and so are not exempt

See Chapter 7 Section 2.8 of your Study Text

81. **C** Arranging the receipt and transmission of orders and managing investments are both core activities. Advising and custody services are classified as ancillary services

See Chapter 1 Section 5.4 of your Study Text

82. **D** All three are required when treating a retail client as an elective professional client

See Chapter 7 Section 1.6.4 of your Study Text

83. **B** The basic aims would include controlling or punishing directors rather than removing their responsibilities, and protecting creditors rather than shareholders of the company

See Chapter 3 Section 4.2.2 of your Study Text

84. **B** A protected disclosure is provided where the regulator requests information. All of the others are market abuse offences

See Chapter 6 Section 5 of your Study Text

85. **B** These four statements are all within the power of the FCA when exercising and carrying out their information gathering and investigatory powers

See Chapter 5 Section 5.2 of your Study Text

PRACTICE EXAMINATION 3

(85 questions in 1 hour and 40 minutes)

Questions

1. In Stock Exchange guidance on the release of price-sensitive information, where a release is lengthy, prominence must be given to

    A   Changes in directors

    B   Details of directors' executive share option schemes

    C   Current and future trading prospects

    D   Material interest disclosure

2. The category of retail investment products most closely defines the range of products on which advice will be provided by

    A   An adviser offering independent advice

    B   An adviser offering restricted advice

    C   An adviser offering basic advice using pre-scripted questions

    D   A product provider

3. The Bank of England has responsibility for the prudential regulation of the following, except which one?

    A   Recognised Investment Exchanges

    B   Securities settlement systems

    C   Recognised Clearing Houses

    D   Recognised payment systems

4. What is the main area of responsibility of the Financial Policy Committee?

    A   Prudential regulation of systemically important financial institutions (SIFIs)

    B   Macro-prudential policy

    C   Monetary policy

    D   Regulation of firms' conduct

5. Which principle would a firm mainly be breaching if it practised churning?

    A   Customers' interests

    B   Financial prudence

    C   Client assets

    D   Skill, care and diligence

6. **Which of the following is not correct of a Recognised Overseas Investment Exchange?**

   A Membership does not confer authorisation to do regulated activities

   B Membership provides a market place in which buyers and sellers may trade

   C They are recognised by the Treasury

   D They regulate the conduct of participants towards each other

7. **A firm does not have adequate systems for compliance oversight. With which of the FCA Principles for Businesses is it failing to comply?**

   A Customers' interests

   B Financial prudence

   C Management and control

   D Skill, care and diligence

8. **Which of the following promotions are permissible?**

   I   A phone call to a retail client who has asked you to call about a particular product

   II   An unsolicited call to market a high volatility investment to a retail client

   III   An unsolicited call to market an investment to an investment professional

   A I only

   B I and III only

   C I, II and III

   D III only

9. **Which of the following is not a permitted investment under the Trustee Act 2000?**

   A 10% of the fund in UK listed equities

   B 10% of the fund invested in overseas land

   C 60% of the fund invested in fixed income securities

   D 60% of the fund invested in regulated unit trusts

10. **Which of the following is not correct in respect of unwritten financial promotions outside the firm's premises?**

    A They may be conducted at any time of day

    B The person communicating it must identify himself and his firm

    C The person communicating it must clarify if the client wants to continue or terminate the communication

    D If an appointment is made, then a contact point must be given to the client

11. **An investment fund wishes to make a financial promotion. Given that the fund has been available for seven years, which of the following are required?**

    I   They must quote performance for at least the last five years

    II   They must attach a statement saying that past performance is no guarantee of future performance

    III They must provide a comparison of performance by similar funds

    A   I only

    B   I and II only

    C   II and III only

    D   I, II and III

12. **Which of the following is not a requirement of SYSC?**

    A   Apportionment of responsibilities so that they can be monitored and controlled by directors

    B   Allocation of one or more individuals in the functions of dealing with the apportionment and overseeing the establishment of systems and controls

    C   Maintaining appropriate systems and controls

    D   The firm must always have a separate compliance function

13. **When assessing suitability in the course of giving advice to a professional client, the firm needs, as a minimum, to take account of**

    A   Investment objectives only

    B   Investment objectives and financial position only

    C   Investment objectives and knowledge and experience only

    D   Investment objectives, financial position and knowledge and experience

14. **Which of the following is true of member firms of the London Stock Exchange?**

    A   They must quote firm prices in those securities in which they deal as principal

    B   They are obliged to register as market makers

    C   They may only act as principal for some securities and agent for others

    D   They can act as either agent or principal in different transactions

15. **Insider dealing legislation does not apply to**

    A   Trades on NYSE Liffe

    B   Trades in OTC interest rate derivatives

    C   Trades in Government bonds

    D   Trades on the LSE

16. Erica has recently passed an appropriate examination and is employed as an adviser by Deancourt Financial Advisers. Erica's friend Azin studied the same exam with Erica and is an adviser with Beardown Advisers. During a social event, Azin tells Erica that one of her clients, Colin, has been repeatedly critical of the service he receives from Beardown. Azin does not know that Colin also has an account with Deancourt, and Erica does not mention this. After checking with her supervisor what are the best terms she can offer but without disclosing her conversation with Azin, Erica offers Colin lower fees if he uses Deancourt for all his financial planning needs. Erica's supervisor learns of the situation and intends to raise the matter with Deancourt's Compliance Department. Which of the following is correct?

A Erica should be commended for taking into account Beardown's weak position

B Deancourt should tell Colin that the confidentiality of information was breached

C Deancourt should write to Colin and ask whether he is dissatisfied with the service provided by Beardown

D Deancourt should ask the Financial Ombudsman whether any complaint has been made by Colin

17. Someone would be guilty only of secondary insider dealing if

    I   They are in possession of insider information

    II   They know it to be from an inside source

    III They have the information through their office, vocation or profession

A I only

B I and II only

C I, II and III

D I and III only

18. Normal settlement for equities through the London Stock Exchange is

A T + 3

B T + 1

C T + 5

D T + 2

19. The regulator refers to certain functions within firms as controlled functions. Such functions are required to be filled by persons who are approved by the regulator.

Which of the following statements is least correct regarding the regime of approved person status and controlled functions?

A Each authorised firm must have an approved person who carries out the significant management function

B A shadow director who carries out required functions will require the approval of the regulator

C An individual's qualifications will be considered by the regulator in the process of evaluating an individual's application for approved person status

D An investment adviser who gives advice on investments and manages investments for clients requires approved person status because these roles are within the customer function

20. **A firm must provide to the regulator, twice-yearly, a report containing (for the reporting period) information about**

    I   The total number of complaints received

    II   The total number of complaints closed

    III   The total number of complaints known to have been referred to and accepted by the FOS

    IV   The total number of complaints outstanding at the end of the reporting period

    A   I and II only

    B   I, II and III only

    C   I, II and IV only

    D   I, II, III and IV

21. **The FCA may impose all of the following penalties for market abuse, except**

    A   An unlimited fine

    B   Issue of a public statement of misconduct

    C   Restitution order against an authorised firm

    D   Apply to the court to impose a custodial sentence

22. **How frequently must an open uncovered derivative position be reported to a retail client?**

    A   Every week

    B   Every two weeks

    C   Every month

    D   Every six months

23. **Which of the following is false regarding whistleblowing procedures?**

    A   Rules and guidance are set out in SYSC

    B   The rules relate to the Public Interest Disclosure Act 1998

    C   Whistleblowing would cover making disclosures relating to criminal offences or damage to the environment

    D   A firm can exclude the employees' whistleblowing rights in their contract of employment

24. **Which of the following is not one of the FCA Principles for Businesses?**

    A   Financial prudence

    B   Best execution

    C   Management and control

    D   Clients' assets

25. **Which of the following disciplinary measures can be used by the FCA?**

       I   Private warnings

       II   Fines

       III   Public statements of misconduct

       IV   Cancellation of permission

A I only

B II, III and IV only

C I, II and III only

D I, II, III and IV

26. **Dealing commission can be used to pay for**

       I   Informed research

       II   Dedicated phone lines

       III   Execution services

A I only

B I and II only

C I and III only

D I, II and III

27. **The LSE is able to conduct investment business. It is correct to state that the LSE is**

A Authorised by the FCA

B Authorised by the PRA

C Given special powers by the Department for Business, Innovation and Skills

D Exempt from authorisation

28. **Edgar Hughes-Willard has been studying the ethical requirements of the regulatory in the retail financial services sector. He has discovered that, as a retail financial adviser, he will need to hold a Statement of Professional Standing (SPS) if he wants to give independent or restricted advice after the end of 2012.**

The SPS will be issued by

A The Prudential Regulation Authority

B The Financial Conduct Authority

C The Financial Services Skills Partnership

D A body accredited by the FCA and subject to FCA oversight

29. **Which of the following is not a specified investment under FSMA 2000?**

    A   Gilt repos

    B   Spot FX

    C   Deposits

    D   Spread betting

30. **Under the client money rules, what best describes a situation where a firm leaves some of its own money in a client money account?**

    A   Pollution of client money account

    B   Pollution of trust

    C   Account in excess

    D   Unreconciled account

31. **Which of the following is false of an institution's responsibilities and liability under anti-money laundering legislation?**

    A   It must establish internal reporting procedures

    B   It must establish identification procedures for customers, except for one-off transactions of a value less than €50,000

    C   It must establish appropriate educational programmes for all relevant employees

    D   Where a firm has not established the required internal systems, then the firm will be committing a criminal offence if money laundering takes place. The penalty is a maximum of two years' imprisonment and an unlimited fine

32. **A fund manager has managed a fund for ten years. When creating an advertisement on the fund, which of the following are requirements of the financial promotion rules?**

    I   Performance must be shown for the last five preceding years

    II   State the reference period and source of the information

    III   Show against performance of similar investments

    A   I and III only

    B   I and II only

    C   II only

    D   III only

33. **Which are true of the German Bund?**

    I   Trades on the German Stock Exchange or OTC

    II   Maturity of 1-5 years

    III   Pays coupon every six months

    A   I and II only

    B   II and III only

    C   I only

    D   I, II and III

34. **What, in relation to MiFID, would be deemed to be a 'large undertaking'?**

    A €20m balance sheet, €20m net turnover

    B €20m balance sheet, €40m net turnover

    C €20m balance sheet, €1m own funds

    D €40m balance sheet, €30m net turnover

35. **Who may a firm not treat as an agent when representing his client, in respect of Designated Investment Business or Ancillary Services?**

    A Another authorised firm

    B An overseas financial institution

    C Another person, provided duties to the agent's client are not avoided

    D Another person where the nature of the relationship between that person and his client is not clear

36. **What distinguishes the concepts of 'suitability' and 'appropriateness' in respect of investment advice?**

    A There is no difference as they are both required protections for retail clients

    B 'Suitability' involves making a personal recommendation and this is not necessarily the case with 'appropriateness'

    C 'Appropriateness' applies only to professional clients

    D 'Suitability' only applies to dealing in derivatives or warrants for a retail client

37. **Which are correct in relation to SETS?**

    I   Orders are matched electronically

    II   It is order driven

    III   It is quote driven

    A I and III only

    B I and II only

    C II only

    D III only

38. **Who arranges stocklending in the Eurobond market?**

    A CREST

    B Clearstream and Euroclear

    C LSE

    D ICMA

39. **What is the rate of stamp duty reserve tax on UK share transfers?**

   A ½% on the consideration

   B 1% on the consideration

   C 2% on the consideration

   D ¼% on the consideration

40. **Which of the following are true of the market abuse regime?**

   I   The offences cover various insider dealing activities and distorting the market

   II   Only regulated firms and their employees are subject to the regime

   III The FCA can penalise anyone for abusive behaviour

   IV   The FCA can oblige authorised firms who have behaved abusively to make good losses to customers

   A I, II and IV only

   B I and IV only

   C I, III and IV only

   D III and IV only

41. **A non-taxpayer receives a net dividend of 10p per share on 500 shares. How much tax, in pounds and pence, can the investor reclaim?**

   Important! You should enter only the answer in numbers (without spaces, letters or symbols) strictly using the following format: 00.00

   ┌─────────────────────────────┐
   │   │
   └─────────────────────────────┘

42. **What is the rate of corporation tax for Spenser Watts plc, a company that earned total profits of £3,650,000 in FY 2012?**

   A 30%

   B 24%

   C 20%

   D 10%

43. **In what currency is an ADR traded?**

   A US dollar

   B Sterling

   C Australian dollar

   D Euro

44. **Which of the following incurs stamp duty on purchase?**

      I   UK registered share

      II   UK bearer share

      III   Options on UK registered share

A I only

B I and III only

C I and II only

D I, II and III

45. **Which of the following statements are correct?**

      I   Defined benefit schemes promise a pension related to the final salary of the participant

      II   Defined contribution schemes carry greater risk to the individual

      III   Defined contribution schemes are sometimes referred to as Money Purchase schemes

A I and II only

B I and III only

C II and III only

D I, II and III

46. **Equity market makers on the London Stock Exchange**

A Must quote prices for a maximum volume of shares up to which they are obliged to deal

B May quote prices for a maximum volume of shares up to which they are obliged to deal

C Must quote prices for a maximum volume of shares but have discretion as to whether they shall deal

D May quote prices for a maximum volume of shares and have discretion as to whether they shall deal

47. **A house is bought for £87,000. What will be the stamp duty land tax payable by the buyer?**

A Nil

B £870

C £1,740

D £2,610

48. **An individual dies leaving an estate of £353,000 to his children. How much inheritance tax is payable?**

A £136,000

B £11,200

C £16,000

D Nil

49. **Lifetime transfers are subject to inheritance tax**

A   If paid within three years of death

B   If paid within five years of death

C   If paid within seven years of death

D   If paid within nine years of death

50. **Consider a firm of independent financial advisers. Which of the following would you not expect to be included in a 'terms of business' letter sent to clients?**

A   The regulator of the firm

B   The charges involved

C   Details of to whom any complaint should be addressed and where to contact them

D   The FCA Principles for Business

51. **Which of the following is not one of the objectives of a fact find?**

A   Determine personal information

B   Determine ethical preferences

C   Determine the level of diversification

D   Determine hard facts

52. **What is the purpose of an investment policy statement?**

I   To detail the stocks that the fund will hold

II   To specify the asset allocation the fund will use

III   To specify market timing options

A   I and II only

B   I and III only

C   II and III only

D   I, II and III

53. **Which of the following most closely describes a real liability?**

A   A liability that grows in real terms as we experience negative inflation

B   A liability that remains static in real terms as we experience positive inflation

C   A liability that shrinks in real terms as we experience positive inflation

D   A liability that remains static in real terms as we experience zero inflation

54. **Which of the following are parts of the FCA Handbook?**

     I   Decision Procedure and Penalties Manual

     II   Supervision

     III   Regulation of Professionals

     IV   Principles for Businesses

A I, II and IV only

B II and IV only

C III and IV only

D I and III only

55. **How many weeks after receiving a complaint should a complainant be informed of their right to use the Financial Ombudsman Service?**

A Four weeks

B Six weeks

C Eight weeks

D Ten weeks

56. **What type of fund is not permitted under the UCITS III Product Directive?**

A Derivatives

B Gold

C Money market

D Warrants

57. **In a general meeting, what is required to demand a poll vote, according to Companies Act rules?**

A Shareholders representing 10% of voting share capital

B Shareholders representing 5% of voting share capital

C Three shareholders

D Only the Chairman can call for one

58. **Which of the following is true of an ordinary power of attorney?**

A The ordinary power of attorney applies on the incapacity of the donor

B The power may not be revoked by the donee

C The power will cease on the death of the donee

D The ordinary power of attorney may not be given as a trustee

59. **Which of the following statements is true for an investor receiving dividends on ordinary share investments, who is not liable to income tax?**

   A   He will be paid gross dividends by the company

   B   He will be paid dividends net of a 10% tax credit but can claim a refund of tax from the company

   C   He will be paid dividends net of a 10% tax but can claim a refund of tax from HMRC

   D   He will be paid dividends net of a 10% tax and cannot claim any refund

60. **For how long after a merger transaction is made public is it possible for the OFT to investigate?**

   A   One month

   B   Three months

   C   Four months

   D   Six months

The following information relates to questions 61 to 66

Milburn plc are a medium sized manufacturing company who have established an occupational pension scheme for their workers. The workers' pay in 7% of their wages to the scheme, and the scheme promises to pay a pension on retirement which is based on the number of years worked and the salary of the worker in their last three years of employment.

61. **Which of the following best describes the style of scheme being operated by the company?**

   A   Defined contribution

   B   Money purchase

   C   stakeholder pension

   D   Defined benefit

62. **Which UK regulator is responsible under the Pensions Act for regulating work-based pensions such as this one?**

   A   OPRA

   B   The Pensions Regulator

   C   The FCA

   D   The OFT

63. **Members of this pension scheme will be given specific information regarding the investment of money held within the scheme. What name is given to this document?**

   A   SIP

   B   Deed of title

   C   Trust deed

   D   TIP

64. **How often is the document described in 63. above required to be published and sent to fund members?**

   A   Monthly

   B   Semi-annually

   C   Annually

   D   As required

65. **Were the company to be unable to meet their obligations, what scheme established under the Pensions Act 2004 could offer protection to members?**

   A   FSCS

   B   FOS

   C   Pension Protection Fund

   D   Pension Compensation Scheme

66. **Under the scheme mentioned in 65. above, what would be the maximum compensation offered to the employees who are not yet retired, as a percentage (%) of their pension payments due?**

   Important! You should enter only the answer in numbers (without spaces, letters or symbols) strictly using the following format: 00

   [   ]

67. **Stamp duty land tax is payable by**

   A   The buyer and the seller

   B   The buyer or the seller

   C   The buyer

   D   The seller

68. **What is the nil rate band for inheritance tax?**

   A   £8,105

   B   £10,600

   C   £300,000

   D   £325,000

69. **An individual dies leaving an estate on £866,000, half of which is paid to his children with the remainder paid to his spouse. How much inheritance tax is payable?**

   A   £211,200

   B   £48,000

   C   £43,200

   D   Nil

70. **Which of the following are real liabilities?**

    I   Loan

    II   Index-linked pension

    III   School fees

  A I and II only

  B I and III only

  C II and III only

  D I, II and III

71. **Which of the following are soft facts in a fact find?**

  A Details of credit card liabilities

  B Details of risk tolerance

  C Details of outstanding mortgages

  D Details of children's ages

72. **What is the best description of capital risk?**

  A Potential variability of inflation rates

  B Potential variability of interest rates

  C Potential variability of current fund values

  D Potential variability of future fund values

73. **Who would normally prosecute a firm for conducting unauthorised regulated activities?**

  A The Department for Business, Innovation and Skills

  B The LSE

  C The FCA

  D The Treasury

74. **Nedra Alexander is a financial analyst with ABC Brokerage Company. She is preparing a purchase recommendation on F & H Corporation. Which one of the following situations would least likely represent a conflict of interest that should be disclosed?**

  A Alexander is on retainer as a consultant to F & H Corporation

  B Alexander's brother-in-law is a supplier to F & H Corporation

  C ABC holds a substantial common stock position of F & H Corporation for its own account

  D Through a family trust Alexander has material beneficial ownership of F & H Corporation

75. **Which of the following is not one of the main money laundering offences?**

   A   Assistance

   B   Tipping off

   C   Fraudulent transaction

   D   Failure to report

76. **Where a person knowingly participates in money laundering, what is the maximum prison term they may face in a criminal court?**

   A   2 years

   B   5 years

   C   7 years

   D   14 years

77. **Where an employee of an authorised firm suspects that money laundering is being carried out by a client, to whom should they report this?**

   A   The MLRO

   B   The CEO

   C   Supervisor

   D   The National Crime Agency (formerly the Serious Organised Crime Agency)

78. **Which of the following are set out as offences under the Terrorism Act 2000?**

   I   Use and possession

   II   Fund raising

   III   Funding arrangements

   IV   Money laundering

   A   I only

   B   II and III only

   C   I, II and III only

   D   I, II, III, and IV

79. **Which of the following is not a possible penalty for the offence of market abuse?**

   A   Unlimited fine

   B   Six months prison sentence

   C   Restitution order

   D   Public statement

80. **Which two of the following penalties may the FCA impose for breaching the market abuse offence?**

    I Maximum fine of £5,000

    II Seven years' imprisonment

    III Public censure

    IV Discipline of approved persons

    A I and II

    B II and III

    C II and IV

    D III and IV

81. **Which of the following instruments does insider dealing legislation cover?**

    I FTSE Index futures

    II Warrants

    III Contracts for difference

    A I and III only

    B II and III only

    C I and II only

    D I, II and III

82. **The maximum penalty for insider dealing when convicted in a Magistrates' Court is**

    A Seven years' imprisonment or an unlimited statutory fine

    B Seven years' imprisonment and an unlimited statutory fine

    C Six months' imprisonment and a £5,000 statutory fine

    D Two years' imprisonment and an unlimited statutory fine

83. **An investment bank GDS plc carries out a number of activities relating to its client Bella plc. GDS acts as Bella's corporate broker. It expects to give advice on a possible merger of Bella with Colleen Baker plc, a listed company which is not a client of GDS. GDS Bank has a market making business unit which makes a market in the stock of Bella plc.**

    In the context of its relationships with Bella plc, what is the main purpose of information barriers that GDS plc may have in place?

    A To restrict the flow of confidential information to the press

    B To enable disclosure of conflicts of interest

    C To prevent personal account dealing by employees

    D To enable GDS to carry on its various types of business

84. **Suspected money laundering transactions should usually be reported to the**

   A   Bank of England

   B   Serious Fraud Office

   C   Stock Exchange

   D   Serious Organised Crime Agency / National Crime Agency

85. **The UK life office, AB Assurance, has initiated a programme to move its call centres to Asia. In doing so, AB is most accurately described as taking advantage of**

   A   Technological advances

   B   Free trade

   C   Regulatory arbitrage

   D   Domestic regulatory pressure

Answers

1. **C** When an announcement is lengthy, LSE guidance is that prominence should be given to current and future trading prospects

    See Chapter 2 Section 4.2.1 of your Study Text

2. **A** An independent adviser will need to provide unbiased, unrestricted advice based on a comprehensive and fair analysis of the relevant market. To reflect the range of products that a consumer would expect an independent adviser to have knowledge of, the regulator has introduced the term 'retail investment product'

    See Chapter 7 Section 8.2 of your Study Text

3. **A** RIEs are regulated by the FCA. The other options (B, C and D) are financial market infrastructures and fall under Bank of England supervision

    See Chapter 2 Section 3.4 of your Study Text

4. **B** The FPC addresses issues of financial stability and resilience at the 'macro' level – that is, at the level of the economy and the financial services sector and sub-sectors

    See Chapter 4 Section 1.7 of your Study Text

5. **A** The firm would be in breach of the customers' interests principle

    See Chapter 8 Section 1.2 of your Study Text

6. **C** They are recognised by the FCA, not the Treasury

    See Chapter 2 Section 3.1 of your Study Text

7. **C** The management and control principle requires firms to have adequate risk management systems, which would include adequate systems for compliance oversight

    See Chapter 8 Section 1.2 of your Study Text

8. **B** Under COBS, where a private customer has requested the call it is allowable. An unsolicited call to market a high volatility investment to a private customer would not be allowable. An unsolicited call to market an investment to an investment professional would be allowable because the investment professional is exempt from protection provided by s21 and COBS

    See Chapter 7 Section 2.13 of your Study Text

9. **B** Overseas land is not a permitted investment under the Act

    See Chapter 4 Section 6.2 of your Study Text

10. **A** Such communications may only be conducted at an 'appropriate' time of day

    See Chapter 7 Section 2.13 of your Study Text

11. **B** There is no requirement to show performance against that of similar funds

    See Chapter 7 Section 2.11.2 of your Study Text

12. **D** It may or may not be appropriate for the firm to have a separate compliance function

    See Chapter 4 Section 5.3 of your Study Text

13. **D** The suitability rules require firms to take account of the client's knowledge and experience, financial position and investment objectives. However, when advising a professional client the firm is entitled to assume that the clie nt has the necessary experience and knowledge in that particular area. Therefore, the firm would only need to take account of the client's investment objectives and financial position

See Chapter 7 Section 3.1 of your Study Text

14. **D** LSE member firms are not obliged to quote firm prices unless they have registered as market makers. Nor are they obliged to register as market makers. They have dual capacity which gives the ability to act as principal or agent in different transactions

See Chapter 2 Section 1.4.5 of your Study Text

15. **B** An OTC interest rate derivative would not be covered by the CJA 1993

See Chapter 6 Section 5.1 of your Study Text

16. **B** This is an ethical matter. Azin has acted unethically by confiding in Erica about her client's affairs, and Erica has acted unethically in acting on that information. Deancourt is free to offer competitive terms to clients in an effort to bring in more business, but in this case it did so based on information it had received following a breach of confidentiality. An ethical approach could involve disclosing this breach to the client

See Chapter 9 Section 2 of your Study Text

17. **B** For the purposes of the legislation a person has information, as an insider, if he knows it is from an inside source and knows that it is inside information (ie price sensitive). These suggest being guilty of 'secondary' insider dealing. If they have information from their own office or employment, that is described as 'primary' insider dealing

See Chapter 6 Section 5.2 of your Study Text

18. **A** In 2001, settlement changed from T + 5 to T + 3

See Chapter 2 Sections 2.1 of your Study Text

19. **A** The significant management function will only need to be present occurs in larger firms, where there is a layer of management below the governing body, which has responsibility for a significant business unit, such as equities, fixed income and settlements in an investment bank. In smaller firms, the governing function will cover the necessary roles

See Chapter 6 Section 1 of your Study Text

20. **D** All this information is required.Note: Although D is the best answer, firms must in fact only report any complaints that have not been resolved by close of business on the business day following receipt of the complaint

See Chapter 6 Section 8.8 of your Study Text

21. **D** The market abuse regime is a civil penalty regime with no risk of imprisonment

See Chapter 6 Section 6.1 of your Study Text

22. **C** Via a periodic statement, which must be sent out at least monthly

See Chapter 6 Section 3.3 of your Study Text

23. **D** A firm cannot exclude an employee's whistle blowing rights

    See Chapter 4 Section 5.8 of your Study Text

24. **B** This is a conduct of business rule rather than one of the Principles for Businesses

    See Chapter 8 Section 1.2 of your Study Text

25. **D** Disciplinary measures available to the FCA are private warnings, public statements of misconduct, fines and variation or cancellation of permission

    See Chapter 5 Section 5 of your Study Text

26. **C** Dealing commission can only be used to buy meaningful research and execution services. Dedicated phone lines are no longer permitted

    See Chapter 7 Section 7.5 of your Study Text

27. **D** The LSE is exempt from the need to be authorised by the regulator: it is instead 'recognised' – as a recognised investment exchange (RIE)

    See Chapter 2 Section 3.1 of your Study Text

28. **D** Professional bodies will be able to obtain FCA accreditation and issue the SPS to their adviser members

    See Chapter 10 Section 1.7 of your Study Text

29. **B** Foreign exchange is not a specified investment under FSMA 2000

    See Chapter 4 Section 4.11 of your Study Text

30. **B** Client money should be segregated from firm's money

    See Chapter 7 Section 6 of your Study Text

31. **B** One-off transactions may be excluded when below €5,000, not €50,000

    See Chapter 6 Section 4.4 and 4.5 of your Study Text

32. **B** There is no need to show against the performance of similar funds

    See Chapter 7 Section 2.11.2 of your Study Text

33. **C** Bunds are generally issued with a maturity of up to ten years. They pay an annual gross coupon and trade both on the German stock exchange and OTC

    See Chapter 2 Section 7.6.2 of your Study Text

34. **B** A large undertaking has €20m balance sheet, €40m net turnover

    See Chapter 7 Section 1.6.4 of your Study Text

35. **D** Where the relationship between a person and his client is unclear, that person cannot be treated as an agent

    See Chapter 7 Section 1.7 of your Study Text

36. **B** Suitability involves making a personal recommendation and this is not necessarily the case with appropriateness

    See Chapter 7 Section 3.3 of your Study Text

37.   **B**   SETS offers electronic trading and is an order matching system. It is not quote-driven as it has no market maker involvement

See Chapter 2 Section 1.1.5 of your Study Text

38.   **B**   The International Capital Market Association (ICMA) regulates the Eurobond market. Clearstream and Euroclear facilitate stock lending

See Chapter 2 Section 7.8.3 of your Study Text

39.   **A**   ½% rounded to the nearest 1p. Stamp duty is ½% of the consideration, rounded up to the next £5

See Chapter 11 Section 6.2.2 of your Study Text

40.   **B**   I is true

II is false: the regime applies to the behaviour, regardless of whom is involved

III is false: the FCA would need to apply to a court to penalise unauthorised persons

IV is true

See Chapter 6 Section 6 of your Study Text

41.   **00.00**No tax can be reclaimed by a non-taxpayer

See Chapter 11 Section 1.3.5 of your Study Text

42.   **B**   The main rate (24% in FY 2012) applies to companies with 'augmented' profits (ie total profits plus gross dividends) of £1,500,000 or more in their chargeable accounting period

See Chapter 11 Section 7.3 of your Study Text

43.   **A**   American Depository Receipts (ADRs) trade on both the NYSE and LSE

See Chapter 2 Section 7.2 of your Study Text

44.   **A**   Stamp duty does not apply upon the purchase of the call option – it only applies if the call option is exercised

See Chapter 11 Section 6.2 of your Study Text

45.   **D**   All of these points are true

See Chapter 10 Section 3.2 of your Study Text

46.   **A**   An equity market maker must quote prices of shares up to a maximum volume, based upon a pre-determined transaction size, known as the Exchange Market Size (EMS)

See Chapter 2 Section 1.1.7 of your Study Text

47.   **A**   Stamp duty land tax is not payable on purchases for this amount

See Chapter 11 Section 6.1.2 of your Study Text

48.   **B**   Inheritance tax is payable at 40% on the value of the estate above the tax free limit, currently £325,000

See Chapter 11 Section 4.7 of your Study Text

49.   **C**   Lifetime transfers within seven years of death are liable to inheritance tax

See Chapter 11 Section 4.7 of your Study Text

50. **D** Details of the regulator need to be included as do the remuneration of the adviser and information about where complaints should be directed. The FCA's Principles for Business would not normally be included

See Chapter 7 Section 1.9 of your Study Text

51. **C** In a fact find, the fund manager will be looking to determine facts about the client, not about his fund

See Chapter 10 Section 2.5 of your Study Text

52. **C** Investment policy statement concentrates on strategic asset allocation and tactical asset allocation (market timing)

See Chapter 10 Section 2.7 of your Study Text

53. **B** A real liability rises with inflation

See Chapter 10 Section 2.3 of your Study Text

54. **A** There is no sourcebook called Regulation of Professionals

See Chapter 5 Section 2.2 of your Study Text

55. **C** After eight weeks, the complainant must be given the FOS leaflet and told of their right to use the service, a right they have a maximum of six months to take up

See Chapter 6 Section 8.5 of your Study Text

56. **B** Tangible assets are not covered

See Chapter 1 Section 6 of your Study Text

57. **A** By s321 CA 2006, any five or more members, or the holders of at least 10% of the voting rights, can demand a poll

See Chapter 2 Section 5.8 of your Study Text

58. **C** The ordinary power of attorney will cease at the end of a specified time, when a specific act has occurred or when the donee dies or becomes incapacitated. To extend decision making beyond this a lasting power of attorney may be needed

See Chapter 3 Section 1.5 of your Study Text

59. **D** The 10% tax credit is 'notional' and cannot be reclaimed

See Chapter 12 Section 1.4 of your Study Text

60. **C** The Office of Fair Trading (OFT) can investigate four months from when the transaction is made public

See Chapter 4 Section 2.4 of your Study Text

61. **D** The other alternatives all refer to similar forms of pension where no guaranteed return is paid but rather it is the value of the fund at retirement which decides the returns paid

See Chapter 4 Section 7.1 of your Study Text

62. **B** The Pension Regulator replaced OPRA in 2005

See Chapter 4 Section 7.2 of your Study Text

63. **A** Statement of Investment Principles – known as the SIP

See Chapter 4 Section 8.1 of your Study Text

64. **C** The SIP must be sent to members annually

See Chapter 4 Section 8.10 of your Study Text

65. **C** The PPF offers compensation if the sponsoring employer becomes insolvent and is unable to pay its liabilities

See Chapter 4 Section 7.3 of your Study Text

66. **90** Where a sponsoring employer becomes insolvent and unable to pay its liabilities, the Pension Protection Fund (PPF) will provide compensation up to 100% of benefits to existing pensioners and up to 90% of benefits to those who have not yet retired

See Chapter 4 Section 7.3 of your Study Text

67. **C** Stamp duty land tax is payable by the buyer of a property

See Chapter 11 Section 6.1.1 of your Study Text

68. **D** The nil rate band for inheritance tax is £325,000

See Chapter 11 Section 4.7 of your Study Text

69. **C** Inheritance tax is not payable when the estate passes to a spouse or civil partner. The half of the estate transferred to the children is taxable to the extent that it exceeds the tax-free band. [(£866,000 ÷ 2) − 325,000] × 40%

See Chapter 11 Section 4 of your Study Text

70. **C** A loan is a nominal liability

See Chapter 10 Section 2.3 of your Study Text

71. **B** Risk tolerance is a soft fact, the others are objective hard facts

See Chapter 10 Section 2.5 of your Study Text

72. **C** The risks described are, respectively, inflation risk, interest rate risk, capital risk, shortfall risk

See Chapter 11 Section 2.6.1 of your Study Text

73. **C** The FCA will prosecute for breaches of Section 19 FSMA

See Chapter 4 Section 4.2.2 of your Study Text

74. **B** According to Standard VI.A – Disclosure of Conflicts, all potential conflicts of interest must be disclosed. The more obvious conflicts of interest are special relationships between a member and the member's firm or an issuer, underwriter or others with financial relationships, such as broker-dealer market-making activities, and positions involving material beneficial ownership of stock

See Chapter 9 Section 1.3 of your Study Text

75. **C** The offence of money laundering refers to the proceeds of crime rather than the crime itself.

See Chapter 6 Sections 4.6 of your Study Text

76. **D** The maximum penalties for any offence of assisting a money launderer are 14 years' imprisonment and/or an unlimited fine when tried in a Crown Court. If tried in a Magistrates Court the maximum penalty is 6 months' imprisonment and a £5,000 fine

See Chapter 6 Sections 4.6.1 of your Study Text

77. **A** The money laundering reporting officer would be the appropriate reporting point

See Chapter 6 Sections 4.10.5 of your Study Text

78. **D** The Terrorism Act 2000 sets out the offences of: fund raising for terrorism; use and possession of money or property for the purpose of terrorism; funding arrangements; and also money laundering

See Chapter 6 Sections 4.11.2 of your Study Text

79. **B** Market abuse is a civil offence, and as such will not carry a prison sentence

See Chapter 6 Sections 6.8 of your Study Text

80. **D** The fine is unlimited. As market abuse is a civil offence, there is no jail sentence available. As an FCA rule would have been broken, an approved person could face FCA disciplinary action

See Chapter 6 Section 6.8 of your Study Text

81. **D** Insider dealing legislation covers equity, debt and related products, such as depository receipts, warrants, derivatives, contracts for differences and all tradable debt instruments, but not collective investment schemes, life insurance policies or commodities such as currency or gold

See Chapter 6 Section 5.1 of your Study Text

82. **C** Had the question asked about the maximum penalty in the Crown Court, the answer would be seven years and an unlimited fine

See Chapter 6 Section 5.7 of your Study Text

83. **D** Information barriers, or 'Chinese walls', can serve to insulate different business units from each other, thus managing potential conflicts of interest that might otherwise lead to GDS having to restrict or to withdraw from certain types of business

See Chapter 9 Section 2 of your Study Text

84. **D** The MLRO would report to the SOCA, if the offence was related to money laundering

See Chapter 6 Section 4.7.3 of your Study Text

85. **A** The internet has made outsourcing of call centre operations more feasible, since documents and messages can easily be transmitted fast around the globe

See Chapter 1 Section 1 of your Study Text

PRACTICE EXAMINATION 4

(85 questions in 1 hour and 40 minutes)

Questions

The following information relates to questions 1 to 3

George Hague has run up a number of personal debts, including an unsecured debt of £690 to Happy House Casino. He also owns GH Ltd which is a small private consultancy in the form of a private limited company which has done only minor business recently. For the past six months, George has had a low income and has found himself unable to pay his debts as they have been demanded.

1. **Given that action is taken leading to George being made bankrupt, which of the following is least true?**

    A   His assets will be transferred into a trust which is used to pay off as much debt as possible

    B   GH Ltd will also be made bankrupt

    C   The Insolvency Act 1986 is key relevant legislation in relation to his bankruptcy

    D   George's financial affairs are taken over by a court

2. **A petition has been made for a bankruptcy order. Which of the following are correct?**

    I   Happy House Casino may have brought the petition

    II   The petition may allege that George has very little prospect of being able to pay his debt

    III   The petitioner may have shown that a statutory demand for payment remains unpaid within two weeks.

    IV   The petitioner may show that a judgement debt has been returned unsatisfied

    A   II and IV only

    B   I and III only

    C   I, II and IV only

    D   II, III and IV

3. **When the bankruptcy order is made, the official receiver takes control of George's assets. Which of the following statements is incorrect?**

    A   The official receiver is an official of the Department of Business, Innovation and Skills

    B   The official receiver is an official of the court

    C   The trustee in bankruptcy protects the bankrupt's property until the official receiver takes over

    D   The bankruptcy of George will begin on the day that the order is made

4. **Natasha is a customer who asks for access under the Data Protection Act 1998 to data held in respect of her personal pension plan.**

   Which of the following responses to the Natasha's request is correct?

   A 'The Data Protection Act entitles you to access to such data and requires that the product provider supplies this information free of charge'

   B 'You may obtain access to the data, but we are permitted to make a charge of up to £2'

   C 'You may obtain access to the data, but we are permitted to make a charge of up to £10'

   D 'The Data Protection Act does not entitle you to access to data relating to personal pension plans'

5. **Which of the following conditions does not necessarily apply to a firm processing personal data?**

   A Data must have been obtained lawfully and fairly

   B Data shall not be processed unless one of the Data Protection Act Schedule 2 conditions is met

   C The data subject must have given consent to the processing of the data

   D Data must not be held longer than is necessary for its lawful purpose

6. **What is the minimum number of shareholders required as a quorum for a listed company to hold an Annual General Meeting?**

   A Two

   B Five

   C Ten

   D One

7. **Inheritance tax on Marilyn's estate is calculated as £50,500. She has already paid lifetime tax on a gift of £60,500. How much is reclaimable by her estate?**

   A £10,000

   B £60,500

   C £50,500

   D Nil

8. **Where will details of directors' transactions in a listed UK company appear?**

   I   Annual Report

   II   Regulatory Information Service

   III Register of Directors' Interests

   A I only

   B I and II only

   C II and III only

   D I, II and III

9. Martin is 80 years old. He has always lived in the UK and has been retired for sixteen years. Martin's wife died last year; Martin has two children and one grandchild. Martin's permanent home is in Scotland, where he owns his own home. Orlando is single. He has lived in England for three years, but his permanent home is in the USA.

    On which of the investments below, if held by each of these individuals, would Martin be subject to UK tax, while Orlando would not, in the event of death?

    A A collection of foreign coins held in a safe deposit box at a London bank

    B Principal private residence in the UK

    C Shares listed on the London Stock Exchange

    D A vacation home in Spain

10. Willard is a securities dealer who has been instructed by private client managers within his firm to buy shares in a particular listed company for a number of clients of the firm. The order is partially filled. The CFA Institute Standards of Professional Conduct indicate that Willard should allocate the stock

    A Randomly

    B In proportion to the amount of commission paid by each client

    C Giving priority to higher-performing accounts

    D In proportion to the order size relating to each client account

11. Steve, an IT consultant, is working for a firm and comes across some price-sensitive information. He is also a shareholder of this company and has already placed a sell order on their shares. Under which of the following circumstances is he not guilty of market abuse?

    A He leaves the sell order

    B He phones a friend and tells them to buy the shares on NASDAQ

    C He buys some more securities

    D He buys more securities, having informed the firm's compliance officer

12. Which of the following is or are true of a proxy vote?

    I   Able to vote in a poll

    II   Able to vote on a show of hands

    III Must be appointed in writing

    A III only

    B I and II only

    C II and III only

    D I, II and III

13. Mrs Okiro buys some shares in X plc for £50,000 and some shares in Y plc for £40,000. In the same tax year, she sells the shares in X plc for £70,000 and the shares in Y plc for £35,000. If Mrs Okiro's marginal rate of tax on gains is 28% and the CGT allowance is £10,600, calculate the capital gains tax payable.

A £2,700

B £1,044

C £1,232

D £2,320

14. Within what period of time must a firm inform the FCA if a person ceases to perform a controlled function?

A 7 business days

B 14 business days

C 21 business days

D 28 business days

15. Within what time frame is a public company required to hold an Annual General Meeting?

A Within three months of the financial year-end

B Within six months of the financial year-end

C Within nine months of the financial year-end

D Not more than fourteen months since the previous AGM

16. Insider dealing is an offence under the

A Criminal Justice Act 1994

B Companies Securities (Insider Dealing) Act 1983

C Financial Services and Markets Act 2000

D Criminal Justice Act 1993

17. One of the conditions for a merger to qualify for referral to the Competition Commission is where the merged company has a market share of more than

A 25%

B 30%

C 40%

D 50%

18. A gift made on the event of a civil partnership from a parent may be made up to how much and still be exempt from IHT?

A Zero

B £1,000

C £5,000

D £10,000

19. **Which of the following has the highest income tax allowance in the fiscal year 2012/13?**

    A   A 40 year old parent of three children who earns £155,000 pa net taxable income

    B   A 66 year old man earning a £15,000 pa pension income

    C   A 25 year old earning £20,000 pa net taxable income

    D   A 76 year old earning £35,000 pa net taxable income

20. **The normal method of issuance for UK government bonds is**

    A   By Dutch auction

    B   By variable price auction

    C   A 'tap' into the secondary market

    D   A tender offer

21. **Where the FCA has refused to grant a Part 4A permission to a firm, then the firm can take their complaint**

    A   To the FCA

    B   To the Financial Ombudsman Service

    C   To HM Treasury

    D   To the Tax and Chancery Chamber of the Upper Tribunal

22. **Which of the following are classified as specified investments under the Financial Services and Markets Act 2000?**

    I   Shares in a US company

    II   Exchange-traded futures

    III   A euro currency option

    IV   Property

    A   I only

    B   I and II only

    C   I, II, III and IV

    D   I, II and III only

23. **A non-taxpayer receives a dividend of £100 from a UK company having had 10% tax deducted. What is the value of tax rebate the investor can claim from HMRC?**

    A   Nil

    B   £10

    C   £12.50

    D   £20

24. **Which of the following is the main piece of legislation which endows the Financial Conduct Authority with its statutory powers?**

   A   Financial Services Act 2010

   B   Criminal Justice Act 1993

   C   Financial Services and Markets Act 2000

   D   Financial Services Act 1986

25. **A house is sold for £562,000. What will be the stamp duty land tax payable by the seller?**

   A   Nil

   B   £8,610

   C   £1,111

   D   £5,740

26. **What is the normal settlement convention for Eurobonds?**

   A   T + 1

   B   T + 2

   C   T + 3

   D   T + 7

27. **One of the categories into which clients may be allocated is 'eligible counterparty'. Which of the following rules will apply to the firm's relationship with eligible counterparties?**

   A   Client agreements

   B   Appropriateness

   C   Best execution

   D   Client categorisation

28. **Which of the following are examples of packaged products?**

   I   Units in a regulated collective investment scheme

   II   Execution only dealing services

   III   Investment trust savings scheme

   A   I and II only

   B   I and III only

   C   II and III only

   D   I, II and III

29. **With respect to a shareholder submitting a proxy voting form to the company, what is the maximum time period that a company may stipulate that the proxy form should be submitted before the AGM, under Companies Act rules?**

   A   Not later than 24 hours before the AGM

   B   Not later than 48 hours before the AGM

   C   Not later than 7 business days before the AGM

   D   Not later than 14 business days before the AGM

30. **Various of your colleagues have become aware of the Retail Distribution Review. You have been asked to prepare a briefing document for staff on the RDR requirements on competence for individuals carrying out retail activities, and on the RDR standards of ethical behaviour.**

   Which of the following is it most correct for your briefing to state?

   The regulator seeks to ensure that retail investment advisers adhere to ethical standards from 2013 onwards through

   A   A requirement to hold a Statement of Professional Standing that will be issued by the regulator

   B   A requirement to hold a Statement of Professional Standing that will be issued by an accredited body

   C   A requirement that advisers follow a Code of Ethics for Investment Advisers that will be published by the FCA

   D   A requirement that advisers follow a Code of Ethics for Investment Advisers that will be published by the Financial Skills Partnership

31. **A four-level approach was used to create a single market in financial services in Europe. What was the process called for introducing a wide range of new legislation?**

   A   EMU

   B   Financial Services Action Plan

   C   Lamfalussy Plan

   D   CESR

32. **Who makes a power of attorney?**

   A   The attorney

   B   The donee

   C   The settlor

   D   The donor

33. **Where are lasting powers of attorney registered?**

   A   The Attorney General

   B   Magistrates Court

   C   Office of the Public Guardian

   D   HM Treasury

34. **Which of the following circumstances is not one which a firm is required to notify to the regulator?**

    A   An adviser has failed to meet agreed persistency levels for contracts arranged with clients

    B   An adviser who has been assessed as competent is no longer considered competent

    C   An adviser has failed to attain an appropriate qualification within the prescribed time limit

    D   An adviser has failed to comply with a Statement of Principle in carrying out his/her controlled function

35. **When an individual's financial affairs are taken over by the court, under the Insolvency Act 1986 this is known as**

    A   An individual voluntary arrangement

    B   Bankruptcy

    C   Insolvency

    D   Liquidation

36. **One of the categories into which clients may be allocated is 'professional client'.**

    In order to be treated as a professional client, a retail client must be all of the following, except

    A   Experienced and knowledgeable

    B   In receipt of a warning

    C   A 'high net worth' individual

    D   Willing to provide a written statement that they are aware of consequences

37. **With regard to the Principles for Businesses, to whom does the term 'customer' refer?**

    A   Retail clients only

    B   Eligible counterparties only

    C   Professional clients and eligible counterparties only

    D   Retail clients and professional clients only

38. **Who is empowered to assess the competence and capability of a person performing a controlled function for an incoming French firm providing MiFID investment services in their Edinburgh branch?**

    A   Scottish regulator

    B   FCA

    C   French regulator (AMF)

    D   FCA and French regulator

39. **Which of the following Statements of Principle for approved persons only apply to significant influence functions?**

    A   Skill, care and diligence

    B   Integrity

    C   Proper standard of market conduct

    D   Comply with regulatory requirements

40. **Which of the following investments provide tax-free income for UK-resident tax payers?**

    A   National Savings Guaranteed Income Bonds

    B   National Savings Investment Accounts

    C   NS&I Savings Certificates

    D   Traded endowment policies

41. **Ken Wong is preparing to give independent investment advice, and is reviewing his knowledge of the range of retail investment products. Which of the following does not fall within the definition of retail investment products?**

    A   100 shares in an open ended investment company

    B   100 shares in a FTSE 100 company

    C   100 units in an unregulated collective investment scheme

    D   100 shares in an investment trust company

42. **Which of the following are requirements of a trustee under the Trustee Act 2000?**

    I   A trustee must normally obtain and consider proper advice

    II   A trustee must have regard to the suitability of the investment to the trust

    III   A trustee has a general duty to exercise reasonable care in investments

    IV   A trustee must review the investments of the trust regularly

    A   I, II, III and IV

    B   I, II and III only

    C   II and III only

    D   I, III and IV only

43. **Where do Japanese government bonds trade?**

    A   Osaka Stock Exchange

    B   JASDAQ

    C   Tokyo Stock Exchange

    D   Over-the-counter

44. **Which of the following is required for an individual to attain threshold competence as a retail investment adviser?**

    I   Passing an appropriate examination

    II   Passing an internal assessment

    III Working unsupervised for three months

    IV Obtain sponsorship from an approved person

    A I, II and III only

    B I and II only

    C I, II, III and IV

    D I and IV only

45. **Which of the following are true regarding the disclosure of directors' interests in shares?**

    I   All dealings must be disclosed to the company

    II   Shareholdings must be disclosed when they pass 1%

    III Disclosure to the company must be within four business days

    A I only

    B II only

    C I and III only

    D II and III only

46. **Which one of the following is not covered by insider dealing legislation?**

    A Debentures

    B Foreign exchange transactions

    C Shares

    D Bonds

47. **If a firm fails to send out a confirmation notice, which of the following Principle for Businesses has been breached?**

    A Integrity

    B Client assets

    C Management and control

    D Communications with clients

48. **If a firm is involved in 'churning' a customer's portfolio, which one of the following Principles for Businesses has most significantly has been breached?**

    A Management and control

    B Financial prudence

    C Customers' interests

    D Client assets

49. **How often should the Statements of Investment Principles be received by an Occupational Pension Scheme?**

    A   Every six months

    B   Every year

    C   Every three years

    D   Every five years

50. **Which of the following is the abbreviation for the French government bond?**

    A   JGB

    B   T-Bond

    C   BOBL

    D   OAT

51. **For a transaction that is undertaken for a retail client on Tuesday 3 April**

    A   It must be confirmed by telephone by the end of the business day

    B   A confirmation must be sent by 4 April

    C   A confirmation must be sent when the customer requests it

    D   The compliance officer will retain all confirmation notes

52. **The statement of investment principles for a pension fund should be written by the**

    A   Pension regulator

    B   Trustees of the pension fund

    C   Sponsor of the pension fund

    D   Company secretary

53. **How long can a share be traded special ex-div prior to the ex-div date?**

    A   Five business days

    B   Ten business days

    C   Fifteen business days

    D   Twenty business days

54. **German equities that have traded on a domestic German equity exchange will settle through**

    A   CREST

    B   Euroclear

    C   Clearstream

    D   EUREX

55. An investor sells £20,000 worth of shares. Which of the following must be paid?

        I   Broker's commission

        II   Stamp Duty Reserve Tax

        III   Takeover Panel levy

A I, II, and III

B I only

C I and II only

D I and III only

56. A UK company authorised by the FCA to advise on investments wishes to offer custodial services. The company should

A Apply to extend its current authorisation

B Notify the Financial Conduct Authority by letter

C Do nothing, as authorisation covers all regulated activities

D Re-apply to the regulator for Part 4A permission

57. An investor buys some shares in Company A for £40,000 and Company B for £30,000. These are then sold within the same fiscal year for £52,500 (Company A) and £29,000 (Company B). If the annual exemption is £10,600, and the investor is a basic rate taxpayer with taxable income of £21,000, what is the capital gains tax payable in £?

Important! You should enter only the answer in numbers (without spaces, letters or symbols) strictly using the following format: 0000

58. For the purposes of the Financial Promotions Order, a high net worth individual is defined as someone with

A Net income of £100,000 or more, or net assets of £250,000 or more

B Net income of £200,000 or more, or net assets of £300,000 or more

C Net assets of £400,000 or more

D Net assets of £500,000 or more

59. **Which of the following statements about the various European Directives are correct?**

    I   The European Directives require each Member State to amend their own law, through the implementation of primary legislation, in order to comply

    II   The European Directives must be implemented by the Member State by the specified date

    III   Each Member State is free to decide whether to implement the European Directive, or to retain their existing legislation

    IV   The European Directives seek to harmonise the various regulations in order to create a fair market place

  A I and IV only

  B I, II and IV only

  C III and IV only

  D I and II only

60. **Client money can best be defined as**

  A Money which the firm looks after, but which is not its own

  B Money from the proceeds of a trade

  C Money which the client deposits with the firm for payment of its fees

  D Interest payable to all customers

61. **Philip, a financial adviser, discovers that his firm has charged some of its clients a fee that is 0.3% higher than that specified in client agreements. The discrepancy has affected approximately 100 of the firm's clients. Philip has spoken with a Senior Manager in his firm. The Senior Manager said that he would ensure that the Accounts Department charges the correct amount for all future work. He does not propose to take any action to correct the past over-charging. From an ethical viewpoint, what action should Philip take?**

  A Do nothing, as the Senior Manager has higher authority within the firm

  B Contact anonymously the clients who have been over-charged

  C Prioritise the financial and competitive position of the firm by accepting and keeping confidential the Senior Manager's decision

  D Make a disclosure to the regulator under the 'whistle blowing' procedure

62. **The price movement for gilts is based on**

  A Eighths of £1

  B Sixteenths of £1

  C Thirty-seconds of £1

  D Decimals of £1

63. **Which of the following is exempt from authorisation?**

  A Broker dealing in government bonds

  B Third party custodian

  C Depositary of an OEIC

  D Appointed representative

64. **UK corporation tax is charged on**

    I   UK profits of UK resident companies

    II   Overseas profits of UK resident companies

    III UK profits of companies resident overseas

    IV Overseas profits of companies resident overseas

  A I, II, III and IV

  B I, II and III only

  C I and II only

  D I only

65. **Which one of the following will be considered as client money?**

  A Client's cash used for settlement of a transaction following a purchase of units in a Unit Trust

  B A remittance, part of which is fees due to the firm

  C Money held in a deposit account with a bank

  D Gold coins held for the value of the metal

66. **What obligation is imposed on a firm by the best execution rule?**

  A To find the current best price and deal at that price

  B To base commission rates on the current best price

  C To advise clients if the price is likely to rise or fall significantly subsequent to a transaction

  D To give best advice on a transaction

67. **An individual dies leaving an estate of £5m to a UK charity. How much inheritance tax is payable on the estate?**

  A Nil

  B £1,875,200

  C £1,880,000

  D £468,800

68. **An investment adviser is likely to consider a liability-driven investment approach for**

    I   Providing for school fees

    II   Repaying a mortgage

    III Investing uncommitted income

  A I and II only

  B I and III only

  C II and III only

  D I, II and III

69. **The rule on inducements**

   A   Prevents authorised firms from making and receiving payments which can lead to avoidance of their duty to the client

   B   Prohibits the firm to receive any payments from third party providers

   C   Requires detailed disclosure of all inducements received

   D   Protects the interests of retail clients only

70. **Which of the following are objectives of a regular investment performance review?**

   I   To determine whether and how client circumstances have altered

   II   To review achieved performance

   III   To consider potential portfolio rebalancing

   A   I and II only

   B   I and III only

   C   II and III only

   D   I, II and III

71. **A firm publishes a quarterly newsletter for their clients. When they make a recommendation about a particular company's shares in the newsletter, the firm is prohibited from**

   A   Including any investment advice in the recommendation

   B   Dealing on their own account until a reasonable time after publication

   C   Giving advice to any client who is affected by a topic covered in the newsletter

   D   Discretionary dealing with any client's assets without specific client instructions

72. **The regulated activities of dealing and managing do not cover**

   A   Shares

   B   Bonds

   C   Warrants

   D   Car insurance

73. **The client money rules are intended to protect, in the event of a firm's insolvency,**

   A   Other investment firms

   B   Shareholders

   C   Bondholders

   D   Customers

74. **Under the Takeover Code, at what percentage of holding must an offer be made?**

   A   20%

   B   30%

   C   50%

   D   90%

75. **Which of the following is a subsidiary of the Bank of England?**

    A The Financial Ombudsman Service

    B The United Kingdom Listing Authority

    C The Financial Conduct Authority

    D The Prudential Regulation Authority

76. **What percentage of shareholders' voting rights is required to back a demand for a poll vote, under Companies Act rules?**

    A 15%

    B 10%

    C 5%

    D 1%

77. **If the FCA wishes to ban a financial promotion that it considers to be misleading then it is empowered to do so**

    A Immediately

    B Only after hearing representations from the firm

    C Only after referring the matter to the Tribunal

    D Only after allowing the firm 14 days to remove the promotion voluntarily

78. **How long does the power of a proxy last?**

    A The day of the AGM

    B The day of the AGM and any adjournment

    C The day of the AGM plus any extension allowed by the Chairman

    D Until the next AGM

79. **The principle of integrity is the first Statement of Principle for Approved Persons. The Code of Practice for Approved Persons (APER) includes various examples of behaviour which would be considered a breach of the statement of this principle. Which of the following is least likely to constitute an example of such behaviour?**

    A Providing false or inaccurate information to the regulator

    B Deliberately aiming to achieve maximum appropriate profits

    C Deliberately failing to disclose the existence of a conflict of interest

    D Misleading others in the firm about the nature of risks being accepted

80. **The FCA has a duty to aim to achieve statutory objectives as laid out by the Financial Services and Markets Act, as amended. It has been suggested that businesses in the financial services sector might aim for the highest ethical standards and in doing so would support these statutory objectives. Which of the following would least well support this suggestion?**

   A   High standards of personal and business behaviour might reduce transparency which would have the effect of reducing Public awareness but increasing confidence

   B   Higher ethical standards would improve the relationship between firm and consumer and thus improve consumer protection

   C   High ethical practices might discourage those who might attempt to launder money from this attempt due to the strong reputation of the financial services industry in that country

   D   High ethical standards would help to differentiate the UK financial services sector as a place of ethical good practice and thus would support market confidence

81. **What is the central purpose of principles-based regulatory approach?**

   A   To encourage firms to adopt a more ethical frame of mind

   B   To shift regulatory focus towards outcomes rather than compliance with detailed rules

   C   To limit the scope for fraud and abuse of power

   D   To secure an appropriate degree of protection for consumers

82. **Where a UK individual dies intestate, and no relative takes an absolute interest, which of the following will take the interest?**

   A   The closest traceable relation

   B   The Crown

   C   HMRC

   D   The FCA

83. **While performing the first client interview, your prospective client asks, 'Why does an adviser undertake a fact find?' You respond as follows.**

   A   To decide whether an investment should be purchased or sold

   B   To enable investment performance to be measured

   C   To enable suitable advice to be given to a client

   D   To enable the facts to be established when a customer has a complaint

84. **Capital risk is best described as**

   A   Potential variability of inflation rates

   B   Potential variability of interest rates

   C   Potential variability of current fund values

   D   Potential variability of future fund values

85. A number of client actions are being considered with respect to money laundering regulations.

John places £30,000 in bank notes into a joint bank account which he has established in the names of himself and his wife.

Brian sells half of his Sainsbury's holding and places it into an investment trust company.

George sells his BP shares and places the funds into a legitimate bank account. He then uses the account to fund legitimate spending.

Which of the following statements is correct?

A John and Brian are both involved in the placement stage

B George is involved in the integration phase

C All are engaging in layering

D Only George is involved in layering

Answers

1.   **B**   As a limited company, GH Ltd would be made insolvent rather than going into bankruptcy which is a term applying to individuals

See Chapter 3 Section 4.1.1 of your Study Text

2.   **A**   The statutory demand should remain unpaid for three weeks for the petition to be appropriate. The court will not entertain a petition from a creditor unless owed at least £750 on an unsecured debt

See Chapter 3 Section 4.1.2 of your Study Text

3.   **C**   This answer is in reverse order: the official receiver hands over to the trustee in bankruptcy

See Chapter 3 Section 4.1.2 of your Study Text

4.   **C**   A charge of up to £10 may be made by the data holder, or £2 in the case of credit reference agency information

See Chapter 4 Section 2.5 of your Study Text

5.   **C**   Although the consent of the data subject is *one* of the Schedule 2 conditions, it is not a necessary requirement except in the case of sensitive personal data

See Chapter 4 Section 2.5 of your Study Text

6.   **A**   A quorum is achieved when two members (or their proxies) are present

See Chapter 2 Section 5.7 of your Study Text

7.   **D**   There is no repayment of lifetime tax paid

See Chapter 11 Section 4.7 of your Study Text

8.   **C**   The annual report details the shareholdings in the company that the directors may have, but not each transaction

See Chapter 2 Section 5.1 of your Study Text

9.   **D**   Martin appears to have UK domicile, while Orlando does not. UK-domiciled individuals are subject to tax on worldwide assets, while non-domiciled individuals will be subject to tax only on UK assets

See Chapter 11 Section 1 of your Study Text

10.   **D**   Section III B of the Standards on Fair Dealing states that members and candidates must deal fairly and objectively with all clients

See Chapter 9 Section 1.3 of your Study Text

11.   **A**   He takes no further action, once he has seen the price-sensitive information

See Chapter 6 Section 6 of your Study Text

12. **D** A shareholder is allowed to attend and vote at a company meeting, however, where the shareholder cannot attend in person, they may appoint a proxy (a third party) to attend in their place. Following CA 2006 changes, proxies may exercise all the powers the member would have if they were present in person, and thus a proxy can vote on a show of hands and on a poll. The proxy granted is valid for that meeting and any subsequent adjournment

See Chapter 2 Section 5.8.5 of your Study Text

13. **C**

	£
Gains in the year (on X plc)	20,000
Losses in the year (on Y plc)	(5,000)
Net gain / loss	15,000
Less: Annual exemption	(10,600)
Amount chargeable to CGT	4,400
£4,900 × 28% =	1,232

See Chapter 11 Section 3 of your Study Text

14. **A** Where an employee of the regulated firm ceases to perform a controlled function then the firm must notify the regulator within seven business days

See Chapter 6 Section 1.2 of your Study Text

15. **B** CA 2006 requires the AGM to be held within 6 months of the financial year-end. Previously, the AGM was required to be held annually and up to 15 months apart

See Chapter 2 Section 5.7.2 of your Study Text

16. **D** Insider Dealing is an offence within Part V of the Criminal Justice Act 1993 (CJA 93)

See Chapter 6 Section 5.1 of your Study Text

17. **A** A 'qualifying merger' is one where the combined companies would control at least a 25% market share in the market concerned. The 'public interest' condition would also be where the turnover of the company being taken over is more than £70m

See Chapter 4 Section 2.4 of your Study Text

18. **C** Gifts to children of up to £5,000 are permitted on their marriage of civil partnership

See Chapter 11 Section 4.5.2 of your Study Text

19. **B** Someone aged 65-74 with below £25,400 in income will be entitled to an additional income tax allowance of £10,500, The 76 year old earning £35,000 will only get the basic personal allowance of £8,105

See Chapter 11 Section 1.4 of your Study Text

20. **B** A variable price auction is otherwise known as a 'competitive auction', where the bidder, if successful, will pay the price he bid. A Dutch auction is another description for a tender method of issuance. The Dutch auction method of issuing government bonds is the approach favoured by the US government when issuing US T-bonds

See Chapter 2 Section 7.3.2 of your Study Text

21. **D** Part 4A permission is with reference to authorisation by the regulators. Part 4A permission is granted by the regulator where the firm satisfies the threshold conditions, and is granted for a particular regulated activity. The level of permission (authorisation) will specify the activities and investments that the firm is authorised in. Permission may be varied by the regulator, or even cancelled, where the regulator has serious concerns about the firm. If the firm wishes to appeal against a decision made by the regulator, then they may appeal to the Tribunal (TCCUT)

See Chapter 5 Section 3.4 of your Study Text

22. **D** Property is not a classification of specified investment under FSMA 2000. Shares in any worldwide company are investments, as are exchange-traded futures and currency options. Other investments that are not covered as regulated investments include land, antiques and various commodities

See Chapter 4 Section 4.11 of your Study Text

23. **A** Investors cannot claim back this implied tax credit. This is also known as the 10% tax credit, which is not reclaimable from the HMRC. The dividend received by the shareholder is treated as the net dividend, net of the 10% tax credit

See Chapter 11 Section 1.3.5 of your Study Text

24. **C** The Financial Services and Markets Act (FSMA) 2000 is the main Act, and was amended by the Financial Services Act 2012

See Chapter 4 Section 1.4 of your Study Text

25. **A** Stamp duty land tax is payable by the buyer not the seller

See Chapter 11 Section 6.1.2 of your Study Text

26. **C** The International Securities Markets Association (ISMA) require that Eurobonds settle three business days after the trade (T + 3). These may be settled through the two electronically linked settlement agencies of Clearstream and Euroclear, allowing firms to use either settlement system

See Chapter 2 Sections 7.1 of your Study Text

27. **D** All other rules apply to retail and professional clients only

See Chapter 7 Section 1.6 of your Study Text

28. **B** The definition of a packaged product includes units in regulated collective investment schemes, Investment trust saving schemes, Life policies and personal pensions and stakeholder pension schemes

See Chapter 7 Section 5.1 of your Study Text

29. **B** A provision in a company's articles that required the notice appointing a proxy to be lodged with the company more than 48 hours before the meeting would be void

See Chapter 2 Section 5.8 of your Study Text

30. **B** The SPS will be issued by accredited professional bodies. The regulator abandoned an earlier plan to issue its own Code of Ethics for retail investment advisers, although advisers must adhere to the Statements of Principle which apply more broadly to approved persons

See Chapter 2 Section 2.11 of your Study Text

31. **B** The question asks for the process of legislation which was the Financial Services Action Plan. This process used the Lamfalussy Committttee's recommendation to use a four level approach to introduce new legislation. CESR was a committee advising on Level 3

    See Chapter 1 section 4.9.1 of your Study Text

32. **D** The donee or attorney acts for the donor under a power of attorney

    See Chapter 3 section 1.3 of your Study Text

33. **C** LPA's must be registered at the OPG to be effective

    See Chapter 3 section 1.7 of your Study Text

34. **A** The notification requirements (applying from July 2011) do not cover persistency levels, which are a measure of the proportion of contracts that remain in force (ie, have not been cancelled) after a specified time period

    See Chapter 6 section 2.8 of your Study Text

35. **B** The question refers to individuals (bankruptcy) and not firms (insolvency). Do not be fooled by the Insolvency Act 1986

    See Chapter 3 section 4.1.1 of your Study Text

36. **C** There is not a requirement that the client should have a high net worth. Sufficient knowledge or transaction volume may qualify the person

    See Chapter 7 Section 1.6 of your Study Text

37. **D** 'Customers' excludes eligible counterparties

    See Chapter 8 section 1.2 of your Study Text

38. **C** Competence and capability are a home state responsibility not host state

    See Chapter 8 section 3.2 of your Study Text

39. **D** Statements of principle 5 – proper organisation of business; 6 – skill care and diligence in management; and 7 – comply with regulatory requirements apply only to those doing significant influence functions

    See Chapter 8 section 3.2 of your Study Text

40. **C** NSI Savings Certificates and Children's Bonds are tax free

    See Chapter 11 Section 1.2.2 of your Study Text

41. **B** Collective investments can be viewed as a packaged form of investment, while a direct holding in company shares is not and does not count as a retail investment product. Unauthorised (unregulated) collective investment schemes count as RIPs, although they will not often be marketed to retail clients

    See Chapter 7 Section 8.3.2 of your Study Text

42. **A** The main elements of the Trustee Act 2000 are that the trustee exercises a duty of care, reviews the investments on a regular basis, and exercises their investment powers. The Act allows a trustee to make any kind of investment, including land and UK property, subject to the trust deed, having obtained and considered proper advice, and having regard to the investment criteria of the fund

   See Chapter 4 Section 6 of your Study Text

43. **D** This is the best available answer since, although there are several stock exchanges in Japan, around 98% of trading in the Japanese bond market is in the over-the-counter (OTC) market

   See Chapter 2 Section 7.4.2 of your Study Text

44. **B** There is no requirement to obtain sponsorship or work unsupervised. The main requirements are that the individual has passed an appropriate examination and has had an internal assessment to determine that they have the appropriate knowledge and experience

   See Chapter 5 Section 3.3 of your Study Text

45. **C** Persons discharging managerial responsibilities (PDMRs), including directors, must notify the company within four business days of a transaction

   See Chapter 2 Section 5.1 of your Study Text

46. **B** Insider dealing legislation relates to the securities of companies (ie bonds and shares) and thus excludes foreign currencies. Debentures are a form of secured bonds

   See Chapter 6 Section 5.1 of your Study Text

47. **D** Principles for Businesses 7, Communication with Clients. This principle, applying to authorised firms, states that the firm must pay due regard to the information requirements of clients (customers and market counterparties), and communicate with them in a way that is clear, fair and not misleading

   See Chapter 8 Section 1.2 of your Study Text

48. **C** Principle for Businesses 6, Customers' Interests, states that the firm must pay due regard to the customers interests, and treat them fairly. Where the firm is churning a portfolio, ie trading too frequently under the circumstances, this principle is being breached

   See Chapter 8 Sections 1.2 and 8.9 of your Study Text

49. **B** The Statement of Principles, published by the Trustees, should be sent out to members annually

   See Chapter 4 Section 8.10 of your Study Text

50. **D** The OAT is a French government bond is the OAT. The BOBL is a medium-term German bond

   See Chapter 2 Section 7.1 of your Study Text

51. **B** Confirmation notes, unless declined, must be sent no later than the first business day following receipt of confirmation (no later than T + 1)

   See Chapter 6 Section 3.2 of your Study Text

52. **B** The trustees have responsibility for writing the SIP

   See Chapter 4 Section 8.10 of your Study Text

53.   **B**   Shares can trade special-ex in the ten business days prior to the ex-dividend period commencing. Remember that shares commence the ex-dividend period two business days before the books closed date, also known as the 'on register' day

See Chapter 2 Section 2.3 of your Study Text

54.   **C**   The clearing house for German equities. Domestic equities officially settle T + 2 in Germany

See Chapter 2 Section 7.1 of your Study Text

55.   **D**   Stamp Duty Reserve Tax (SDRT) is only paid by the buyer of a UK share that are in an electronic format, ie uncertificated. If an investor bought a certificated share, then they would pay stamp duty rather than stamp duty reserve tax

See Chapter 11 Section 6.2 of your Study Text

56.   **D**   Authorisation is not blanket and firms must apply for Part 4A varying permission to undertake additional regulated activities. The level of permission granted initially will specify the level of regulated activities and investments to which it relates – any variation of this will require the firm to vary their permission level by applying again to the regulator

See Chapter 5 Section 5.3 of your Study Text

57.   **0162**   Company A : Capital Gain = £52,500 – £40,000 = £12,500

                    Company B: Capital Loss = £29,000 – £30,000 = £1,000

                    Net capital gain   £11,500

                    Less: £(10,600) (Annual exemption)

                    Taxable gain: £900

                    Gain taxed @ 18%: Tax payable = $0.18 \times £900 = £162$

See Chapter 11 Section 3 of your Study Text

58.   **A**   A high net worth individual is exempt from s21 of FSMA and the financial promotion rules of the Conduct of Business Sourcebook

See Chapter 7 Section 2.8 of your Study Text

59.   **B**   The various European Directives, such as the MiFID or the Capital Requirements Directive, seek to 'harmonise' regulations in order to create a fair market place. Each Member State is required to amend their own law to comply, either through the introduction of new legislation or through amendments to existing statute

See Chapter 1 Section 4.2.3 of your Study Text

60.   **A**   This is the best definition of client money

See Chapter 7 Section 6 of your Study Text

61.   **D**   The disclosure under the whistle-blowing procedure will be protected under the Public Interest Disclosure Act 1998

See Chapter 4 Section 5.8 of your Study Text

62.   **D**   Gilts are priced using a decimal format

See Chapter 2 Section 1.3 of your Study Text

63. **D** Appointed representatives are exempt persons

   See Chapter 4 Section 4.5 of your Study Text

64. **B** UK resident companies pay corporation tax on their worldwide profits. Non-UK resident companies pay corporation tax on their UK generated profits

   See Chapter 11 Section 7 of your Study Text

65. **B** Only money held in connection with designated investment business will be considered client money, and not the contents of deposit accounts. The rest are the items specifically identified by the regulators as not being client money

   See Chapter 7 Section 6 of your Study Text

66. **A** The firm must deal at the best available price

   See Chapter 7 Section 7.2 of your Study Text

67. **A** Gifts to charities are tax-exempt

   See Chapter 11 Section 4.7 of your Study Text

68. **A** Uncommitted income is, by definition, not targeted towards any commitment, hence will be managed to maximise returns

   See Chapter 10 Section 2.2.1 of your Study Text

69. **A** The rule on inducements protects the interests of all clients. Only summary disclosure of fees/commissions/non-monetary benefits from third party providers are required. Detailed disclosure must be provided on request

   See Chapter 7 Section 7.6 of your Study Text

70. **D** They are all objectives

   See Chapter 10 Section 2.10 of your Study Text

71. **B** They should not deal as the effect of the letter could be to increase the share price. If the company holds the stock, there could be a conflict of interest

   See Chapter 7 Section 4 of your Study Text

72. **D** Car insurance is not covered by the 'dealing' or 'managing' categories. It is covered by 'effecting or carrying out contracts for insurance'

   See Chapter 4 Section 4.6 of your Study Text

73. **D** If client money were not protected, non-segregated funds would be seized by the liquidator and treated as property of the firm

   See Chapter 7 Section 6 of your Study Text

74. **B** 'Effective control' is achieved at 30%, requiring a mandatory offer

   See Chapter 4 Section 3.4 of your Study Text

75. **D** The PRA has been set up as a subsidiary of the Bank of England. The UKLA is a function of the FCA, which is an independent company. The FOS is also an independent entity

   See Chapter 4 Section 1.2 of your Study Text

76. **B** A poll vote may be demanded by shareholders who represent 10% of the voting rights. A poll vote may also be requested by five members, having the right to vote, or by the Chairman. It is also important to note that a proxy may demand, or assist in demanding a poll vote

See Chapter 2 Section 5.8 of your Study Text

77. **A** The regulator is able to give a direction to firms requiring them immediately to withdraw or to modify promotions which it deems to be misleading, and to publish such decisions. The firm is then able to make representations to the FCA to challenge the Authority's decision

See Chapter 1 Section 2.20 of your Study Text

78. **B** A proxy is valid for a given meeting or any meeting to which it is adjourned

See Chapter 2 Section 5.8 of your Study Text

79. **B** The list of examples is long and you would not be expected to learn each example. It is however expected that you be able to recognise behaviour in line with acting with integrity. In this question, aiming to maximise profits seems to be a normal business aim rather than a breach of integrity

See Chapter 9 Section 2.12.2 of your Study Text

80. **A** Higher ethical standards should increase transparency rather than reducing it and as such should improve public awareness

See Chapter 9 Section 2.13 of your Study Text

81. **B** A is the rationale behind the Treating Customers Fairly (TCF) initiative. D is one of the operational objectives of the FCA

See Chapter 9 Section 2.11.2 of your Study Text

82. **B** If no relative takes an absolute interest in the event of an individual dying intestate then the crown takes the interest

See Chapter 3 Section 5.3 of your Study Text

83. **C** The fact find is effectively required to meet the need to 'Know your customer'. Having information about clients enables the adviser to tailor advice to the client's requirements

See Chapter 10 Section 2.5 of your Study Text

84. **C** The risks described are, respectively, inflation risk, interest rate risk, capital risk, shortfall risk

See Chapter 10 Section 2.6 of your Study Text

85. **B** George is involved in the integration phase; John is involved in the placement phase; Brian is involved in the layering phase

See Chapter 6 Section 4.2 of your Study Text

PRACTICE EXAMINATION 5

(85 questions in 1 hour and 40 minutes)

1. An agency agreement exists between a client and their financial advisers. Given that no specific contractual arrangement exists at this stage, which of the following is least likely to be a duty of the agent as implied by law?

    A   The requirement to exercise skill and care

    B   The requirement to keep accounts

    C   The requirement to delegate responsibilities

    D   The requirement to act in good faith

2. A medium-sized firm of independent financial advisers is the subsidiary of a UK-listed parent company. The firm is reviewing its procedures in the light of the Bribery Act 2010. The directors have noted that Ministry of Justice guidance sets out the principle that a commercial organisation's procedures to prevent bribery should be 'proportionate'.

    The requirement of proportionality is best described as meaning that the company's procedures should

    A   Focus on the possibility of instances of bribery that could be material to the financial statements

    B   Be proportionate to the bribery risks it faces and to the nature and scale of the company's activities

    C   Focus anti-bribery efforts on markets and sectors in which bribery is least tolerated

    D   Be proportionate to the levels of bribery that have been experienced in the past by the company and to the complexity of the company's activities

3. What is the maximum penalty in a Magistrates' Court for conducting a regulated activity in the UK while not authorised?

    A   Six months' jail or a fine of £5,000

    B   Six months' jail and a fine of £5,000

    C   Six months' jail or an unlimited fine

    D   Six months' jail and an unlimited fine

4. Which of the following is not one of the threshold conditions that the regulator will evaluate in order for a firm to obtain authorisation from the FCA?

    A   Effective supervision

    B   Business model

    C   Issues and products

    D   Appropriate resources

5. **Which of the following is part of the role of the Bank of England?**

   A   Prudential regulation of investment exchanges

   B   Setting interest rates in the UK

   C   Appointing head of FCA

   D   Setting appropriate inflation targets for the UK

6. **Under MiFID, if an investment firm sets up a branch in another EEA state, to whose local rules will the branch have to adhere?**

   A   Home state

   B   Host state

   C   Home and host states

   D   The branch can choose which rules to follow

7. **Xaviera believes that, 20 months ago, she was mis-sold a retail financial product by a UK financial adviser and made a complaint. The finding of the adviser firm's complaints investigators was that the case was 'without merit' and the firm declined to offer any compensation.**

   12 weeks has passed since Xaviera received the firm's final response to her complaint. Xaviera now plans to refer the complaint to the Financial Ombudsman. Xaviera expects that the Financial Ombudsman's decision will award her compensation of £200,000 excluding costs.

   A   The Financial Ombudsman is not the correct agency to approach in these circumstances

   B   The amount that Xaviera expects to receive exceeds the maximum award available through the Financial Ombudsman

   C   Too long a time period has passed since the event complained about for Xaviera to take her complaint to the Financial Ombudsman

   D   Too long a time period has passed receiving the firm's final response for Xaviera to take her complaint to the Financial Ombudsman

8. **Which of the following are MiFID exclusions?**

   I   Stockbroking firms

   II   Insurance companies

   III   Collective investment schemes

   IV   Credit institutions accepting deposits

   A   I, II, III and IV

   B   None of I, II, III and IV

   C   I, II and III only

   D   II, III and IV only

9. **Under the advice regime applying under RDR rules, an adviser giving independent advice is**

    A   Barred from using panels

    B   Expected to review all markets when considering what is suitable for a client

    C   Barred from accepting commission from a product provider

    D   Required to charge hourly rates for advice given

10. **What is the required delay before trading under the rules on dealing ahead of research?**

    A   The firm must wait until the market price has responded

    B   The firm must allow a reasonable time for the clients to react before placing its own trades

    C   One working day

    D   There is no required delay once the information is public

11. **Which of the following is not a client category under MiFID?**

    A   Professional clients

    B   Eligible counterparties

    C   Retail clients

    D   Intermediate clients

12. **A company director purchases shares in his company, which is listed on the London Stock Exchange. What is the company required to do?**

    A   Inform the market via a Primary Information Provider regardless of his holding

    B   Inform the market via a Primary Information Provider if t takes his holding above 1% of the shares in the company

    C   Inform the market via a Primary Information Provider if it takes his holding above 3% of the shares in the company

    D   There is no requirement for reporting the transaction

13. **If a company proposes to pay a dividend, how should this announcement be handled?**

    A   In a briefing to a select group of analysts

    B   In a notice published in at least one national newspaper

    C   By informing a Primary Information Provider

    D   By sending a circular to all shareholders

14. Which two of the following tests are necessary in order to treat a client as an elective professional client?

    I   Qualitative test

    II Mandatory test

    III Quantitative test

    IV Management test

  A I and II

  B II and III

  C I and III

  D II and IV

15. Which of the following words or phrases is not centrally related to the requirements on communication of financial promotions?

  A Clear

  B Not misleading

  C Reasonable

  D Fair

16. Which of the following are permissible goods and services in connection with the use of dealing commission arrangements?

  A Portfolio valuation services

  B Travel and entertainment costs

  C Computer hardware associated with specialist software

  D Research providing original thought

17. What is the maximum award which can be determined by the Financial Ombudsman Service, excluding costs?

  A £100,000

  B £150,000

  C £250,000

  D Unlimited

18. What is the minimum number of annual report and accounts that a company should have filed prior to application to join the Full List?

  A One year

  B Two years

  C Three years

  D Five years

19. **What is the main purpose of the client money rules?**

    A   To maximise the returns to investors by pooling firm's money with those of clients

    B   To ensure that interest can be divided fairly between accounts

    C   To protect against the insolvency of the firm

    D   To facilitate maximum interest of client deposits

20. **The FCA has the power to prosecute, through the criminal courts, for a number of offences, but not in respect of**

    A   Misleading the regulator

    B   Insider dealing

    C   Market abuse

    D   Breaches of money laundering regulations

21. **If a client has taken a complaint to the authorised firm which has not been resolved in two months, then the next step the client may take to resolve the complaint is to**

    A   Refer the complaint to the Financial Ombudsman Service to decide the case

    B   Refer the complaint to the regulator

    C   Ask the firm to take the complaint to the Tribunal (TCCUT)

    D   Take the complaint to the Financial Services Compensation Scheme

22. **In the context of appropriateness, which of the following statements is true?**

    A   The firm must assess the client's understanding of risk

    B   The rule applies when a client responds to a promotion selling non-complex instruments

    C   The firm must assess the client's financial situation and investment objectives

    D   The firm must not perform a transaction if they have not satisfied themselves that the instrument is appropriate

23. **Who is the primary regulator of the US equities markets?**

    A   SEC

    B   IRS

    C   Federal Reserve

    D   FCA

24. **When a firm provides performance information in relation to MiFID business, to what period must it relate?**

    A   The five preceding years

    B   If the product has been established for less than five years, then only three years data need be used

    C   At least the five preceding years or the whole period of the life of the product if this is less than five years

    D   A 12-month period only

25. **Which of the following is not a hard fact?**

    Details of

    A   A client's state of health

    B   A client's name of address

    C   A client's attitude to risk

    D   A client's tax status

The following relates to questions 26 to 30

Martin Jameson is 80 years old and has been retired for sixteen years. He has a final salary pension. He is married with two children and one grandchild. He and his wife own their own house plus a holiday home in Northumberland belonging to Martin. They wish to prepare plan effectively to minimise their potential inheritance tax outgoings.

26. **At the time when they visit their adviser, Martin is domiciled abroad while his wife is domiciled in the UK. They are correctly advised that the exemption available for tax-exempt transfers from his wife to Martin were she to die would be**

    A   Zero

    B   £55,000

    C   £325,000

    D   Unlimited

---

27. **Assuming that Martin is UK-domiciled, which of the following would not be good advice for him to follow to minimise his IHT liability?**

    A   Make full use of exemptions available

    B   Use life assurance policies

    C   Make PETs before CLTs in the tax year

    D   Make lifetime gifts

---

28. **In order to minimise IHT, Martin gives his holiday home to their children. The parents do however continue to use the house several times a year without paying rent. How would this form of arrangement best be described?**

    A   CTF

    B   PET

    C   CLR

    D   GWR

29. The holiday house which Martin has given to their children but still continues to use rent-free has a value of £500,000 on his death four years after having given up ownership of the house. At the time of the gift, it had been worth £420,000. What sum in £ would be added to Martin's death estate relating to the house on his death?

   Important! You should enter only the answer in numbers (without spaces, letters or symbols) strictly using the following format: 000000

30. Martin's wife dies in June 2012, leaving £162,500 to their children and all other assets to Martin. Were Martin to die in the future, when the nil rate band has changed to £425,000, what available nil rate band (in pounds) would be available to use at that point?

   Important! You should enter only the answer in numbers (without spaces, letters or symbols) strictly using the following format: 000000

31. Who is responsible for sending out a Cancellation Notice?

   A   The product provider

   B   The compliance officer

   C   The investment adviser

   D   The Financial Conduct Authority

32. The CFA Code of Ethics requires members to do all of the following except

   A   Use reasonable care and exercise independent professional judgement

   B   Promote the integrity of capital markets

   C   Avoid excessive remuneration

   D   Act with integrity, competence, diligence and respect

33. Within what period of time must the Competition Commission normally investigate cases following the date of reference?

   A   4 months

   B   24 weeks

   C   3 months

   D   48 weeks

34. **Which of the following would be committing an offence under the Criminal Justice Act 1993 if they purchased shares in ABC plc?**

    I   A market maker who obtained price-sensitive information in the course of his business and the information is of a kind it would be reasonable to expect him to obtain

    II   A director of ABC plc with price-sensitive information who undertook the transaction without intending to make a profit or to avoid a loss

    III A friend of a director of ABC plc who obtained information but was unaware that it was price-sensitive

    IV An employee of ABC who has heard a rumour of an impending takeover bid

    A I, II, III and IV

    B II, III and IV only

    C II and III only

    D None of I, II, III and IV

---

35. **At what rate will a higher rate taxpayer pay capital gains tax on the disposal of an asset giving rise to a gain higher than the annual allowance?**

    A 40%

    B 20%

    C 28%

    D 10%

---

36. **Which of the following is not a direct power of the FCA?**

    A The right to issue principles and general rules

    B The ability to compensate those who have suffered losses from the failure of regulated firms

    C The right to investigate authorised firms or certain employees

    D The power to recognise clearing houses and investment exchanges

---

37. **To which of the following do the insider dealing rules not apply?**

    I   Corporate brokers

    II   Market makers

    III Stabilisation

    A I only

    B II only

    C I and II only

    D II and III only

---

38. **The best execution rule is designed to protect**

    A All investors

    B Retail clients

    C Retail and professional clients

    D Retail and professional clients, but professional clients can opt out

39. **With respect to 'best execution criteria', a firm does not have to take into account**

    A The client, including categorisation as retail or professional
    B The financial instruments
    C The previous day's closing price
    D The execution venues

40. **What is the main benefit to customers of the client money rules?**

    A They require a firm to perform frequent reconciliations of client money
    B They allow one client's overdraft to be netted off against the credit balance of another
    C They keep the customers' money segregated from the firm in the case of collapse of the bank
    D They allow interest to be earned by all customers on their client money accounts

41. **Which of the following are Principles for Businesses applying to all authorised firms?**

    I   Financial prudence
    II   Relations with regulators
    III   Conflicts of interest
    IV   Communication with clients

    A III and IV only
    B I and III only
    C I, II and IV only
    D I, II, III and IV

42. **Ainsworth plc is going into administration. Which of the following best describes the procedure?**

    A The purpose is to provide a better way of realising the company's assets than could be achieved by receivership
    B The administrator is in most cases appointed out of court by a debenture holder
    C The administrator is concerned principally with the interests of the secured creditors who appointed them
    D The administrator acts mainly in the interests of unsecured creditors

43. **The Money Laundering Regulations require a firm to do which of the following activities?**

    I   Perform appropriate identification checks on all new accounts
    II   Keep accurate records of transactions for five years
    III   Provide appropriate training to all staff

    A I and III only
    B I only
    C II and III only
    D I, II and III

44. Which of the following is totally dependent on market returns?

A A defined benefits pension scheme

B A traditional employer-based pension scheme

C A final salary pension scheme

D A defined contribution pension scheme

45. GEMMs and IDBs settle trades in UK government bonds through the

A CGO

B CREST

C LSE

D BOE

46. De Weir plc anticipates that it will earn profits of £160,000 in its financial year ending 31 March 2013. What rate of corporation tax will the company pay?

A 27%

B 26%

C 21%

D 20%

47. In relation to the member states of the European Union, what is the consequence of the issue of a European Directive?

A It automatically becomes law in each member state

B It requires law in each country to be changed by their respective Parliament in accordance with the directive

C It recommends that each state's Parliament introduces laws to implement its proposals

D It becomes law in each member state once approved by the European Parliament

48. Lifetime transfers are subject to inheritance tax

A When paid

B On the death of the transferor

C If paid within seven years of the death of the transferor

D Never

49. Which of the following is incorrect regarding data protection?

A Data protection legislation is set out in the Data Protection Act 1998 (DPA)

B There are eight data protection principles

C Breaches of the DPA are punishable by two years' imprisonment and unlimited fines

D The Act covers electronic or manually stored data

50. **Which of the following terms best describes the approach of the UK Corporate Governance Code and the Stewardship Code?**

    A 'Rules-based compliance'

    B 'Self-regulatory compliance'

    C 'Voluntary compliance'

    D 'Comply or explain'

51. **Which of the following is true of a Multilateral Trading Facility (MTF)?**

    A It is a facility where a firm engages in multiple core investment services

    B It is a system where a firm provides services similar to those of exchanges by matching client orders

    C It is a system where a firm takes proprietary positions with a client

    D It is a facility where a firm operates in more than one location

52. **A house is bought for £875,000. What will be the stamp duty reserve tax payable by the buyer?**

    A Nil

    B £8,750

    C £26,250

    D £35,000

53. **An individual dies leaving an estate on £340,000, half of which is paid to his children with the remainder paid to his spouse. How much inheritance tax is payable?**

    A £136,000

    B £11,200

    C £16,000

    D Nil

54. **A client gives specific instructions for the execution of a trade. In this case, best execution may be waived**

    A For that trade only

    B For all subsequent trades until the client requests best execution again

    C For that category of transactions only

    D Best execution may not be waived

55. A group of clients of Brookmead Advisers have concluded contracts for different product types and have received the contract terms and conditions on the same date – 1 April. Distance selling was not involved. For which products had the cancellation period expired by 24 April?

   A   Personal pension plan

   B   Initial income withdrawal from a stakeholder pension plan

   C   Level term assurance policy

   D   Enterprise Investment Scheme investment

56. Which of the following are real liabilities?

   I   Income provision for dependents

   II   Personal pension

   III   College fees

   A   I and II only

   B   I and III only

   C   II and III only

   D   I, II and III

57. Which of the following are types of investment risk?

   I   Interest rate risk

   II   Shortfall risk

   III   Capital risk

   A   I and II only

   B   I and III only

   C   II and III only

   D   I, II and III

58. The 'decision-specific' test for assessing whether a person has the capacity to take a particular decision at a particular time is set out in the

   A   Mental Health Decisions Act

   B   Mental Capacity Act

   C   Incapacity Act

   D   Financial Services and Markets Act

59. Which of the following is a specified investment?

   A   Premium Bonds

   B   Trade bills

   C   Real estate

   D   T-bills

60. **If the outcome of the Financial Ombudsman investigation is accepted by the complainant, then it is**

    A At the discretion of the firm to comply

    B Implemented by HMT

    C Binding on the firm

    D Binding on the customer

61. **Takeover Panel rules apply to**

    A Listed companies only

    B All public companies

    C Listed companies with a market capitalisation greater than £5 million

    D All public companies with a market capitalisation greater than £5 million

62. **Within what period of time must the OFT make recommendations, following the date that transactions take place?**

    A 4 months

    B 6 months

    C 24 weeks

    D 48 weeks

63. **Martin Power heads the research department of a regional brokerage firm. The firm employs many analysts, some of whom are subject to the Code and Standards. Should Martin delegate some of his supervisory duties, which statement best describes his responsibilities under CFA Institute Code and Standards?**

    A Power is released from responsibility for those duties delegated to his subordinates

    B Supervisory responsibility is retained by Power for all subordinates despite delegation of some of his duties

    C Power may not delegate supervisory duties to subordinates, because of the Code and Standards

    D Power's supervisory responsibilities would not extend to subordinates who are not subject to the Code and Standards

The following relates to questions 64 and 65

Jerome Stanford has recently become employed by Pendleton Willard Asset management as a fund manager. When being inducted into the company, it is explained to Jerome by his supervisor that high ethical standards will be expected of him at the firm.

64. As an approved person in his role as fund manager, Jerome will be governed by the Code of Practice for Approved Persons. Which of the following would least likely be a breach of the Code?

A Knowingly misusing the assets of a client

B Not informing his firm the true risk of the investments he is making for the firm

C Disclosing a conflict of interest between the firm and the client

D Recommending investments to his client which he knows are unsuitable

65. Jerome's supervisor explains to him the importance of acting on behalf of all stakeholders of the firm. Which of the following would be considered stakeholders?

   I   Employees

   II   Clients

   III The general public

   IV   Shareholders

A II only

B IV only

C I, II and IV only

D I, II, III and IV

66. Macro-prudential regulation is best described as falling within the remit of

A The Financial Conduct Authority

B The Financial Policy Committee

C The Prudential Regulation Authority

D The Money Advice Service

67. The Takeover Code applies to acquisitions of

   I   Public companies

   II   Fully listed companies

   III Companies on the AIM

   IV   Private companies

A II only

B II and III only

C I, II and III only

D I, II, III and IV

68. Mrs Rodriguez works for an FCA-authorised firm and wishes to deal in securities on her own account. Which of the following is the best description of the regulations concerning this trade?

A She must notify the stock exchange of her deals

B She should be aware of the personal dealing restrictions and inform her firm promptly of any personal transactions

C She may only deal in products offered by her own firm

D She may not deal in securities

69. **Which of the following require authorisation?**

   I   Tip sheets
   II   Newspaper investment advice columns
   III Introducers
   IV Trustees

   A I and II only
   B I, II and III only
   C I only
   D I, II, III and IV

70. **If an individual loses £40,000 in investments in the event of an authorised firm defaulting, how much compensation will be received from the Financial Services Compensation Scheme?**

   A £30,000
   B £40,000
   C £39,000
   D £36,000

71. **A company has rights as defined by law in its capacity as a legal person. Which of the following best describes its status?**

   A A natural person
   B An artificial person
   C A corporate person
   D A limited person

72. **Which of the following is not subject to the Financial Promotion Rules?**

   A A promotion communicated to a person in the UK
   B A cold call from someone in the UK to someone outside of the UK
   C A promotion in relation to a takeover
   D A promotion issued by an appointed representative

73. **For which client types is a basic written agreement needed?**

   I   Retail client
   II   Professional client
   III Eligible counterparty

   A I only
   B II only
   C I and III only
   D I, II and III

74. **What is the most relevant adjective when considering the amount of protection required for any particular client?**

    A   Proportionate

    B   Appropriate

    C   Relevant

    D   Adequate

75. **Martha Reeves is preparing to give investment advice on an independent basis after the end of 2012, and is reviewing her knowledge of the range of retail investment products (RIPs).**

    Which of the following does not fall within the definition of advice on RIPs?

    A   Martha recommends that a single 30-year old man invests in shares of an open ended investment company

    B   Gemma, who already holds a stocks and shares ISA which includes contributions made only in previous tax years, is recommended by Martha to buy a holding of the ordinary shares of BP plc within an ISA, using contributions to be made in the current tax year

    C   Martha recommends that a retired client buys ordinary shares in Foreign & Colonial Investment Trust plc

    D   Martha gives advice on a Self-Invested Pension Plan that is capable of holding commercial property among its assets

76. **Which of the following is the best execution rule designed to protect?**

    A   Investors generally

    B   Retail clients generally

    C   Retail and professional clients generally

    D   Retail and professional clients, but professional clients can opt out

77. **Which of the following must be provided by a member in a six-monthly portfolio valuation?**

    I   The name of the firm

    II   Each designated investment held and its market value or, if unavailable, its fair value

    III   Total fees and charges

    IV   The cash balance at the beginning and end of the reporting period

    A   I and II only

    B   I, III and IV only

    C   III and IV only

    D   I, II, III and IV

78. **Which two of the following may refer a complaint to the Financial Ombudsman Service as an eligible complainant?**

    I   A private individual

    II   A director of the insolvent firm

    III A small business

    IV   A large company

    A   I and II

    B   II and III

    C   III and IV

    D   I and III

79. **The Tax and Chancery Chamber of the Upper Tribunal (TCCUT) reviews the decisions of**

    A   The FCA only

    B   The FCA and HMT

    C   HMT only

    D   The Bank of England

80. **The conflict of interest policy of a firm is least likely to prevent**

    A   A conflict between the authorised firm and their client

    B   A conflict between the firm and their competitor

    C   A dispute between different divisions within an authorised firm

    D   A dispute between the clients of the firm

81. **You are writing a brief for managers of your firm about the personal account dealing rules.**

    What would be the best statement of the purpose of the rules on personal account dealing?

    A   To prevent dealing when in the knowledge that the firm's research department are about to release a positive report on a security

    B   To prevent dealing in shares owned by the investment company

    C   To prevent dealing in shares when the company's directors have just announced the results

    D   To prevent the firm taking a principal position in securities where there is a conflict of interest

82. **Which of the following statements about rules governing investment research activities is incorrect?**

    A   Financial analysts can take positions in securities contrary to their current recommendations only in exceptional circumstances and with senior permission

    B   Analysts must refrain from dealing on the information contained in research until the clients have been provided with time to consider it

    C   Research analysts must not promise issuers favourable research coverage

    D   The issuer should be permitted to review unpublished research on their company at any time

83. **Which of the following could be used to settle Eurobonds?**

   A Euroclear

   B The SETS system

   C LCH Clearnet

   D The London Stock Exchange

84. **Which of the following is the final part of the financial planning process?**

   A Determining objectives

   B Formulating recommendations

   C Obtaining relevant information

   D Selecting funds

85. **Mr Singh is the holder of 4% of a company's voting shares. He is not the Chairman nor a director of the company. He wishes to demand a poll vote at the company's general meeting. Who else's support along with Mr Singh would be sufficient in order to demand the poll, under Companies Act rules?**

   A Four other shareholders

   B Two other shareholders who hold 1% of the voting shares between them

   C One other shareholder who holds 4% of the voting rights

   D No support is needed from other persons: Mr Singh alone is entitled to call for a poll

Answers

1. **C** The duty of an agent in the absence of an agreement would require that the agent act in person rather than delegate responsibility

    See Chapter 9 Section 2.7 of your Study Text

2. **B** The MoJ guidance states (Principle 1: Proportionate procedures) that: 'A commercial organisation's procedures to prevent bribery by persons associated with it are proportionate to the bribery risks it faces and to the nature, scale and complexity of the commercial organisation's activities. Small organisations may face significant bribery risks, although they are unlikely to need procedures that are as extensive as those of a multi-national organisation

    See Chapter 6 Section 7 of your Study Text

3. **B** The Crown Court penalty is an unlimited fine. This general prohibition is contained within s19 of FSMA

    See Chapter 4 Section 4.2.2 of your Study Text

4. **A** 'Issues and products' is a description of the third pillar of the FCA's supervision model, and is not one of the threshold conditions

    See Chapter 5 Section 3.3 of your Study Text

5. **B** The Bank's Monetary Policy Committee sets benchmark interest rates, as part of its monetary policy role

    See Chapter 2 Section 2.12 of your Study Text

6. **C** If a firm has a physical presence in another EEA country, it must adhere to the local rules of that country for most of the Conduct of Business rules. However, there are a few minor exceptions, such as personal account dealing rules, that follow the home state rules

    See Chapter 1 Section 5.3 of your Study Text

7. **B** The maximum FOS award is £150,000. The FOS is the correct agency, and the complaint is within time limits (6 months since the firm's final response; 6 years since the event, or 3 years since becoming aware of the problem or since the person could reasonably be expected to become aware of it)

    See Chapter 6 Section 9 of your Study Text

8. **D** MiFID exclusions are insurance companies, CISs and credit institutions when they are not providing MiFID services, just accepting deposits

    See Chapter 1 Section 5.5 of your Study Text

9. **C** Panels may be used to help review the market. The firm will not be expected to review markets for products that do not meet a client's needs and objectives. The adviser's charging structure may or may not be based on hourly rates, but commission must not be taken from product providers

    See Chapter 7 Section 8.5 of your Study Text

10. **B** COBS is worded such that firms must provide clients with a 'reasonable opportunity to act'

    See Chapter 7 Section 4 of your Study Text

11. **D** Intermediate clients is not a classification category used in COBS

See Chapter 7 Section 1.6.1 of your Study Text

12. **A** All deals conducted by directors must be announced to the market

See Chapter 2 Section 5.1 of your Study Text

13. **C** It is important for this information to be communicated to the market in a fair and transparent fashion. The company communicates the information to one PIP, who then distributes this information to the market as a whole through quote vendors such as Bloomberg and Reuters

See Chapter 2 Section 5.6 of your Study Text

14. **C** Mandatory test and management test are made up terms. The qualitative test requires experience, expertise and knowledge. The quantitative test requires a certain frequency of transactions, minimum portfolio value or knowledge of transactions from professional work in the financial sector

See Chapter 7 Section 1.6.4 of your Study Text

15. **C** The words used are: fair, clear and not misleading

See Chapter 7 Section 2.4 of your Study Text

16. **D** Only research and goods or services relating to the execution of trades are a permitted use of dealing commission

See Chapter 7 Section 7.5 of your Study Text

17. **B** The maximum FOS award is £150,000, although costs can also be awarded

See Chapter 6 Section 9.5 of your Study Text

18. **C** The company should have filed published accounts covering at least three years

See Chapter 2 Section 4.2 of your Study Text

19. **C** The rules aim to restrict the commingling of client's and firm's money so reducing the risk that clients will have their money absorbed by creditors in the event of a firm becoming insolvent

See Chapter 7 Section 6 of your Study Text

20. **C** Market abuse is a civil offence, not a criminal offence

See Chapter 6 Section 6 of your Study Text

21. **A** This must be referred to the FOS within six months

See Chapter 6 Section 8.8 of your Study Text

22. **A** The aim of the appropriateness check is to determine whether the client has the experience and knowledge to be able to understand the risks involved

See Chapter 7 Section 3.3 of your Study Text

23. **A** The Securities and Exchange Commission is the US regulator. The Federal Reserve (FED) is a distractor, as is the IRS (Internal Revenue Service)

See Chapter 2 Section 6.3 of your Study Text

24. C Information on past performance must include appropriate information covering at least the five preceding years, or the whole period the investment service has been offered/provided, or the whole period the financial index has been established if less than five years

See Chapter 7 Section 2.11.2 of your Study Text

25. C The client's attitude to risk can be regarded as a 'soft' fact

See Chapter 10 Section 2.5 of your Study Text

26. B Gifts between spouses are exempt, if spouses are domiciled in the UK. Where one spouse is non-domiciled, the exemption available on transfers to the non-domiciled spouse is limited to £55,000 (2012/13). The nil-rate band of £325,000 is available in addition to this

See Chapter 11 Section 4.5.3 of your Study Text

27. C The others are all possible advice. Annual exemptions are allocated chronologically during the tax year, however. CLTs are immediately chargeable to IHT so these should be done first to avoid the PETs using up the annual exemptions

See Chapter 11 Section 4.4 of your Study Text

28 D A Gift with Reservation (GWR) would best describe this arrangement

See Chapter 13 Section 3.3 of your Study Text

29. 500000 As Martin continues to use the house rent-free, it would be treated as if it were still part of his estate and its full value at the time of death would be added to his estate

See Chapter 11 Section 4 of your Study Text

30. 637500 The unused portion of Martin's wife's nil rate band would be added to his own nil rate band at his death. This would be (£162,500 / £325,000) × £425,000 plus the rate on death of £425,000 which gives a value of £637,500

See Chapter 13 Section 3.2.2 of your Study Text

31. A The provider should send it out. If the provider omits to do so, the client retains cancellation rights for 24 months

See Chapter 7 Section 5.3 of your Study Text

32. C The CFA Code does not specifically address the issue of remuneration

See Chapter 9 Section 1 of your Study Text

33. B Four months refers to the time limit for the OFT to investigate once transactions are made public

See Chapter 4 Sections 2.3 and 2.4 of your Study Text

34. D Note that as a friend of the director you are only an insider if you 'know' it is inside information. An employee hearing a rumour would not count as information

See Chapter 6 Section 5.3 and 5.4 of your Study Text

35. C CGT for higher rate taxpayers is taxed at 28%

See Chapter 11 Section 3.3.4 of your Study Text

36. **B** The ability to compensate those who have suffered losses from the failure of regulated firms rests with the Financial Services Compensation Scheme (FSCS)

    See Chapter 5 Section 1.2 of your Study Text

37. **D** Market makers and stabilised securities are special defences regarding insider dealing

    See Chapter 6 Section 5.5 of your Study Text

38. **C** The best execution rule is aimed at protecting both retail and professional clients. Professional clients cannot opt out of best execution. The term all investors would include eligible counterparties

    See Chapter 7 Section 7.2 of your Study Text

39. **C** Prices can move dramatically from one day to another so when seeking 'best execution' today, yesterday's price is not relevant

    See Chapter 7 Section 7.2 of your Study Text

40. **C** The main purpose of the client money rules is to segregate the firm's money from client money to prevent and protect in the case of the firm's insolvency

    See Chapter 7 Section 6 of your Study Text

41. **D** All four statements are Principles for Business

    See Chapter 8 Section 1.1 of your Study Text

42. **A** It would better describe the actions of the receiver where a debenture holder appoints them via a court to work on their interests. Acting for unsecured creditors better describes a liquidator

    See Chapter 3 Section 4.1 of your Study Text

43. **D** The Money Laundering Regulations deal with the institutional liability and require a firm to have all of these activities in place

    See Chapter 6 Section 4.5 of your Study Text

44. **D** The risk with a defined contribution pension scheme is very much with the employer. The other three options are different ways of describing the same type of scheme

    See Chapter 10 Section 3.2 of your Study Text

45. **B** Settled through CREST, a dematerialised settlement system

    See Chapter 2 Section 7.1 of your Study Text

46. **D** The small profits rate of Corporation Tax is 20% (Financial Year 2012)

    See Chapter 11 Section 7 of your Study Text

47. **B** It is not effective until the local law has been changed

    See Chapter 1 Section 4.2.3 of your Study Text

48. **C** Lifetime transfers within seven years of death are liable to inheritance tax

    See Chapter 11 Section 4.4 of your Study Text

49. **C** Breaches of the DPA do not result in imprisonment, only fines

     See Chapter 4 Section 2.4 of your Study Text

50. **D** While compliance is not strictly required, companies should explain where they do not comply with the codes

     See Chapter 2 Section 5.4 and 5.5 of your Study Text

51. **B** A multilateral trading facility provides an alternative order matching system to an exchange. The client orders match with other clients so the firm operating the system does not take proprietary positions

     See Chapter 2 Section 1.6 of your Study Text

52. **A** Stamp duty land tax is payable by the buyer, not stamp duty reserve tax

     See Chapter 11 Section 6.1.2 of your Study Text

53. **D** Inheritance tax is not payable when the estate passes to a spouse or civil partner. The half of the estate transferred to the children is covered by the tax-free band

     See Chapter 11 Section 4 of your Study Text

54. **A** When a firm executes an order following specific instructions from the client, it should be treated as having satisfied its best execution obligations only in respect of the part or aspect of the order to which the client instructions relate. The fact that the client has given specific instructions which cover one part or aspect of the order should not be treated as releasing the firm from its best execution obligations in respect of any other parts or aspects of the client order that are not covered by such instructions

     See Chapter 7 Section 7.2 of your Study Text

55. **D** EIS shares carry a 14-day cancellation period

     See Chapter 7 Section 5.3 of your Study Text

56. **D** All are real liabilities, rising through inflation

     See Chapter 10 Section 2.3 of your Study Text

57. **D** All are investment risks

     See Chapter 10 Section 2.6.1 of your Study Text

58 **B** The Mental Capacity Act 2005 sets out a single 'decision-specific' test for assessing whether a person lacks capacity to take a particular decision at a particular time

     See Chapter 3 Section 1.8 of your Study Text

59. **D** Premium bonds are National Savings and Investments products and exempt. Trade bills, such as cheques/other bills of exchange, are excluded from the definition, as is buying real estate or land. Please note that Treasury bills of exchange are regarded as specified investments

     See Chapter 4 Section 4.11 of your Study Text

60. **C** The firm must comply with the Financial Ombudsman's rulings

     See Chapter 6 Section 9.5 of your Study Text

61. **B** The City Code applies to all UK public companies, both listed and unlisted. It also applies to certain private companies where the company has been listed in the last ten years

See Chapter 4 Section 2.1 of your Study Text

62. **A** The normal period is four months from the date that transactions are made public

See Chapter 4 Section 2.4 of your Study Text

63. **B** Under Standard IV.C – Responsibilities of Supervisors, members may delegate supervisory duties to subordinates but delegation does not relieve them of their supervisory responsibilities. Any investment professionals with employees subject to their control or influence are considered to have supervisory responsibilities, and are required to take steps to prevent anyone under their supervision from violating the law or the Code and Standards

See Chapter 9 Section 1.3 of your Study Text

64. **C** Disclosure of the conflict of interest is appropriate behaviour and would not be a breach of the Code

See Chapter 9 Section 2.12.2 of your Study Text

65. **D** The various groups with an interest of some kind in the business and its activities are termed stakeholders and would include all of the above

See Chapter 9 Section 2.13 of your Study Text

66. **B** The FPC is a Committee at the Bank of England, with responsibilities in macro-prudential regulation and in the monitoring of stability and resilience in the financial system

See Chapter 4 Section 1.7 of your Study Text

67. **D** The basic principle of the Code is to protect shareholders. The Takeover Code (or 'City Code') applies to all UK public companies (plc), both listed and unlisted (AIM companies) and to certain private limited companies (Ltd)

See Chapter 4 Section 2.1 of your Study Text

68. **B** As Mrs Rodriguez is an employee of a FCA-authorised firm, to prevent conflicts of interest she must comply with the personal account dealing requirements in her contract of employment

See Chapter 7 Section 7.7 of your Study Text

69. **C** An introducer solely introducing a potential investor to an authorised person, does not constitute arranging transactions even if paid. Trustees will generally only be considered to be conducting investment business if paid for their services, as trustees who do not hold themselves out to the market as providing a service are on the list of excluded activities

See Chapter 4 Section 4.10 of your Study Text

70. **B** If we assume that the question is relating to an investment, then the maximum award per claim would be 100% of the first £50,000, which would result in an award of the full £40,000

See Chapter 6 Section 10.3 of your Study Text

71. **B** The law recognises artificial persons in the form of corporations

See Chapter 3 Section 1.1 of your Study Text

72.   **C**   Communications related to takeovers are subject to the Takeover Code

          See Chapter 7 Section 2.7 of your Study Text

73.   **A**   For a professional client and an eligible counterparty, there is no requirement for an agreement, although most firms will wish there to be one

          See Chapter 7 Section 1.9 of your Study Text

74.   **A**   The word used is 'proportionate'

          See Chapter 7 Section 1.5 of your Study Text

75.   **B**   Directly held shares are not in a packaged form and so are not included within the definition of RIPs. OEIC shares, investment trust shares and SIPPs are all within the definition of RIPs, whether or not the investments are held in an ISA or child trust fund. SIPPs are capable of holding commercial property, subject to the SIPP provider's own rules

          See Chapter 7 Section 8.3.2 of your Study Text

76.   **C**   The best execution rule is aimed at protecting both retail and professional clients. Professional clients cannot opt out of best execution. The term 'investors generally' would include eligible counterparties

          See Chapter 7 Section 7.2 of your Study Text

77.   **D**   All of these are required

          See Chapter 6 Section 3.3 of your Study Text

78.   **D**   A complaint may be dealt with under the Financial Ombudsman Service (FOS) only if it is brought by, or on behalf of, an eligible complainant. An eligible complainant could be a private individual or a small business

          See Chapter 6 Section 8.1 of your Study Text

79.   **A**   The Tax and Chancery Chamber of the Upper Tribunal (TCCUT) will conduct a complete rehearing of FCA enforcement and authorisation cases where the firm or individual and the FCA have not been able to agree the outcome

          See Chapter 5 Section 3.4 of your Study Text

80.   **B**   Regulatory requirements on conflicts of interest aim to protect the interests of the client

          See Chapter 4 Section 5.6 of your Study Text

81.   **A**   This is the best available answer. This is because the personal account dealing rules apply to employee trading where a conflict of interest arises

          See Chapter 7 Section 7.7 of your Study Text

82.   **D**   Pre-publication drafts can be previewed by the issuer only for the purpose of verifying compliance

          See Chapter 7 Section 4.1 of your Study Text

83.   **A**   Eurostream and Clearstream are where Eurobonds are settled

          See Chapter 2 Section 7.1 of your Study Text

84. **D** The other activities must be carried out before selecting the funds in which to invest

    See Chapter 10 Section 2.1 of your Study Text

85. **A** A poll vote may be called by shareholders having 10% of voting rights, or by five members, or by the Chairman

    See Chapter 2 Section 5.8 of your Study Text